AN ABSOLUTE CASSEROLE

THE TASKMASTER COMPENDIUM

ALEX HORNE AND JACK BERNHARDT

QUERCUS

First published in Great Britain in 2024

QUERCUS

An imprint of
Quercus Editions Limited
Carmelite House
50 Victoria Embankment
London EC4Y 0DZ

An Hachette UK company

The authorised representative in the EEA is Hachette Ireland, 8 Castlecourt Centre, Castleknock Road, Castleknock, Dublin 15, D15 YF6A, Ireland

Copyright © 2024 Avalon Television Limited

The moral right of Alex Horne and Jack Bernhardt to be identified as the authors of this work has been asserted in accordance with the Copyright, Designs and Patents Act, 1988.

Picture credits: pp. vi, 9, 14, 59: Simon Webb/ Avalon Television Ltd; pp. viiiix, x, 38, 40–42, 44, 49, 64, 77, 96, 100, 130, 132, 136, 156, 186, 206, 209, 215, 221, 232, 246, 252, 299, 305: Andy Devonshire; p. 27: studio floorplan / James Dillon; pp. 43 and 45 floorplans / Jenny Walker; p. 79: UK map / Shutterstock / hitesh98; p. 89: world map / iStock / Maryia Liubamirskaya; p. 96: paperclip / Shutterstock/ YZ vector; pp.112, 140, 174, 213, 265, 280: egg / Shutterstock/ Pineapple studio; pp.161–164: design of Sausage Studies exam / Andrew Dames; p.178: Taskmaster Education / University of Warwick; p. 276 and plate section: Martin Rosten / Pixel Pie.

All rights reserved. No part of this publication may be reproduced or transmitted in any form or by any means, electronic or mechanical, including photocopy, recording, or any information storage and retrieval system, without permission in writing from the publisher.

A CIP catalogue record for this book is available from the British Library

Designed and typeset by seagulls.net

HB ISBN 978-1-52944-152-9
EBOOK ISBN 978-1-52944-153-6

To my wife Rachel, who has had to see her husband doing things on TV that are far from ideal

Alex

To my wife Valerie, who has had to listen to too many hours of me talking about points inflation

Jack

CONTENTS

1 / Join Our Cult: How It Started — 1

2 / Hell Is Here: Life in the Taskmaster Studio — 15

3 / Little Polythene Grief Cage: A Guide to the Taskmaster House — 39

4 / The Alpine Darling: Taskmaster and the Rest of the World — 65

5 / An Orderly Species: Taskmaster and Society — 101

6 / I've Sinned Again: Taskmaster and Law & Order — 131

7 / No Stars For Naughty Boys: Taskmaster and Education — 157

8 / BMXing!: Taskmaster and Sport — 187

9 / Roadkill Doused in Syrup: Taskmaster and Food — 207

10 / A Coquettish Fascinator: Taskmaster and Fashion — 233

11 / Enormous Hugeness: Taskmaster and Celebrity — 253

12 / A Show About Pedantry: Taskmaster and Language — 277

Index 300

Acknowledgements 307

A WORD FROM THE TASKMASTER

When my assistant whispered to me his plan for this so-called compendium at midnight one Thursday, I closed my eyes, rolled over and barked at him to leave my boudoir. I don't know what he was doing in there in the first place. It's a restricted zone and he will never have the necessary authorisation.

Since that regrettable moment I have softened slightly and am now able to endorse the idea as a fairly worthwhile endeavour, as long as I don't have to get actively involved myself.

On that note, it's worth saying that my assistant has written every one of these words, because I am still in my boudoir with my eyes shut, my arms spread and my feet raised high in their special girdle.

Do not fear. As always, I am across the important details. I made the little man dictate this passage to me (he was instructed to shout it through my window one particularly rainy afternoon) and after four hours I gave him my silent approval.

And so it is that you are now holding this exhaustively researched tome and I am:

Greg Davies
THE TASKMASTER

1

JOIN OUR CULT

HOW IT STARTED

At time of writing, there have been 160 episodes, 789 tasks, 17 champions, 3 champions of champions, 12,409 points given out, 325 disqualifications, approximately 495 rubber ducks and around a metric ton of watermelon juice spilled. But like escalators, age and eggs if you fill them with enough helium, these numbers will only keep going up. There's only one *Taskmaster*, and it keeps marching on.

But how did this cultural behemoth, this chaotic combination of creativity, cruelty and caravans, come to be? Let's make like Greg Davies and dig down into the narrative. This is the story of how *Taskmaster* was born.

A MESSY BIRTH

In May 2009 Alex Horne became a father for the first time. He'd spent every August for the previous ten years telling jokes at the Edinburgh Fringe festival, but this summer he was supposed to stay at home, joyfully cuddling his newborn.

In May 2009 Tim Key became a godfather for the third time. That August, as he had done for the previous ten years, he told jokes (well, poems) at the Edinburgh Fringe festival and enjoyed himself.

While his son slept and gurgled and cried, Alex read his friend's reviews. They were exceptional. But instead of being overwhelmed with both paternal and fraternal pride, Alex was bored and jealous. This was made worse when, towards the end of the month, Tim was nominated for the Edinburgh Comedy Award, the pinnacle of a comedian's career.

The following morning Alex woke up with a fully formed idea in his head. He would return to Edinburgh the following year. And he would bring with him not only his son, but also his own comedy award, a brand-new pinnacle for comedians and one that he would be in charge of.

Before the month was over, Alex had sent an email to twenty comedians, including Tim. It read as follows:

```
Hello,

I know we're in the middle of Edinburgh, but I'm not
there this year so am busily and enviously planning
```

1 / JOIN OUR CULT

for next year. Apologies if I'm adding to your current festival gubbins.

I'm writing to you because I like what you do. In particular, I like the fact that you sometimes do interesting things then tell people about them in a funny way.

Next year I am planning to do a show in Edinburgh celebrating people like you. I don't know what it'll be called yet, but here's the basic idea:

- In August 2009 (now) I write to a small number of the people I admire the most and challenge them to join in the ultimate comics' challenge.

- Over the next year I write to them twelve more times, on each occasion setting them a new and daunting/amusing/pointless/tiny/divvy task.

- At one grand climax (perhaps a couple) in Edinburgh 2010 I reveal the results in a show that will feature as many of the competitors as are able to attend (probably sitting on chairs in a line — ready to explain/defend their actions and query their opponents' technique/honesty).

And also, to reassure you, the tasks that you will be asked to perform won't be too wacky, expensive or time-consuming. On paper, they'll be fairly straightforward. Things like 'Take a picture of yourself with a famous animal' or 'Write an essay on Dickensian women'. And you're encouraged to think laterally (I won't say cheat, but as long as you're not caught cheating, who would know?). You will be asked to submit corroborating evidence to prove you've done what you've said you've done, but it's up to you how you come about this evidence.

It could take as little or as much of your time as you fancy. That's it really. What I'd like you to do now is let me know:

a) If you're at all interested

b) If you think you'll be at Edinburgh next year (not crucial)

Right then. I won't let you know who else I've contacted just yet as it might be nice to have an air of secrecy about the whole competition (it might also be nice to have a league table somewhere, so you can see how you're scoring and who's in the lead, so it's all a bit more dynamic – I'll make decisions like that soon).

For now, goodbye.

And, before I go, don't worry at all if you're not interested, just let me know as soon as you know.
And, of course, if you say you are you can always say you're not later on. OK then.

Bye!

Alex Horne

1 / JOIN OUR CULT

Twenty-four hours later, the following twenty comedians had signed up:*

1. Al Pitcher
2. Dan Atkinson
3. Guy Morgan
4. Henning Wehn
5. Jarred Christmas
6. Joe Wilkinson
7. James Dowdeswell
8. Josie Long
9. Lloyd Langford
10. Lloyd Woolf
11. Mark Olver
12. Mark Watson
13. Mike Wozniak
14. Rick Edwards
15. Steve Hall
16. Stuart Goldsmith
17. Tim Fitzhigham
18. Tim Key
19. Tom Basden
20. Tom Wrigglesworth

* Looking at this list now it is strikingly male and un-diverse, a reflection of my view of the stand-up circuit at the time, perhaps, but more realistically, a demonstration of my own embarrassingly small circle of comedy friends. It goes without saying that *Taskmaster* specifically, but also pretty much everything in life is better with a broader range of people, with more mixed outlooks on life – with variety.

Another twenty-four hours after that, Tim Key won the Edinburgh Comedy Award.

One month shy of six years later, the first episode of *Taskmaster* was broadcast on television. Alex Horne was not in charge.

FROM STAGE TO SCREEN Part 1

Hello.

I'm Alex Horne, I'm 6'2" and little, and you're probably reading this because at some point you have stumbled upon the unlikely story of *Taskmaster*, a tale still being told today.

As explained, the idea was born soon after my first son, who is now nearly as tall as me (I can't stress enough how above average my height is). But the path from birth to sprawling television concept is so unpredictable and precarious that any sort of metaphors become instantly redundant. Let's just say it's been surprising.

The Edinburgh show happened. It was both memorable and swiftly forgotten. We all moved on with our lives. Except I couldn't quite move on with mine, because it was so much fun. And I still had this small child to occasionally escape from.

So the following year, I did the show again. Twelve more tasks, this time for just ten comedians; a more wieldy number. It was so much fun again. And this time Avalon, a television production company, agreed that it was so much fun. They suggested we pitch it to TV stations to see if we could make it for more people. We persuaded Andy Devonshire to join our team. He made *The Apprentice* and *The Great British Bake Off* and, more importantly, liked fun.

We also unanimously and immediately decided that I should *not* be the Taskmaster. You've probably seen me. You'll understand why. I don't have the breadth of shoulders, the weight of voice or the thickness of skin. I'm also not as funny as the man we all knew was the only correct answer to the question, 'Who should be the inaugural

1 / JOIN OUR CULT

Taskmaster, the one to whom all shall answer, the breaker of dreams and creator of champions?'

So I asked Greg. We knew each other from the circuit, although not well enough for me to ask him to be involved in the Edinburgh show. (I'm pretty sure he has since told me that irked him because he felt left outside of my cosy comedy clique. Fair enough. Although it was simply because I was, back then, slightly scared of him.)

Greg said: 'Maybe.'

He wanted to know who the comedians were going to be. I said I'd get back to him.

Meanwhile, I'd started asking comedians.

We needed a big name attached to this project so we started with one of my heroes, a father figure to British stand-up comedy, perhaps the most naturally funny person I've ever encountered (alongside Greg, obviously. And, begrudgingly, Tim Key): Mr Frank Skinner.

Frank said: 'Maybe.'

He wanted to know who the Taskmaster was going to be? I said I'd get back to him.

I got back to Greg first. 'Frank Skinner is up for it,' I said. 'Fine, I'll do it,' said Greg.

I got back to Frank next. 'Greg Davies is doing it,' I said. 'Fine, I'm up for it,' said Frank.

We were off.

STATIONERY ARCHERY
Or HOW ANDY DEVONSHIRE AND I FIRST MET by Alex

Andy and I might have lived together for six weeks in LA back in 2017, making an American version of *Taskmaster* for Comedy Central, while also hiking the Californian mountains, watching whales from the Pacific Coast Highway and drinking tequila with Mexicans on Cinco de Mayo, but this story starts in a soulless office in Ladbroke Grove eight years previously.

It was essentially a blind date. I needed a director, he needed a project, the matchmakers thought we'd click. They were so right.

We were supposed to be making a documentary based on one paragraph hidden in a dusty compendium of forgotten British sports that fleetingly mentioned a game of cricket on horseback. A few months later and we had indeed recreated the event, playing and filming a full-blooded limited overs match with commentary by Blowers himself. Also Andy and I had become firm friends. There's barely been a day in the nine years since on which we haven't spoken.

But it was those hours in that windowless office that I'll always remember. That was the start. How do you begin? Well, instead of picking up a pen or opening a browser, Andy crumpled up a piece of paper. We were sat on a mezzanine level, below us were several desks, a photocopier and, most important of all, a bin.

'I bet I can get it in,' said Andy with confidence and a smile.
'I bet I can get it in,' I replied, making my own paper ball.
We both threw.
We both missed.
We both laughed.

1 / JOIN OUR CULT

We both spent the rest of the day throwing paper balls into that bin. We invented our own sport, our own cricket on horseback.

Instead of earnestly making plans and endlessly trawling the Internet, Andy taught me that having fun is the best way to do good work. While mucking about we got to know each other. We talked while chucking things into things and we got excited about our little film. And we still haven't stopped playing our silly games with our own friends, families and the UK's top comedians. I'm a very lucky person.

'It's a beautiful world,' Andy said every day in LA. It is. That office was drab. But it will always be beautiful in my mind, because I got to share it with Andy D.

TASKMASTER HALL OF GLORY
*Youngest Contestant**

NAME: Lolly Adefope

AGE AT EPISODE TRANSMISSION: A scarcely believable 26 years old

SERIES: 4

POINTS: 125 (2.78 points per task)

POSITION IN SERIES: Fifth, because, as Greg has said, he hates the youth more with every year that passes.

FUN FACT: Lolly has the highest points-per-task score in prize tasks, winning for an adorable baby photo of herself and a picture of herself as Princess Diana. (NB: These were two separate pictures.)

GREATEST ACHIEVEMENT: In a task where she had to move an egg into an eggcup, she did it the quickest, using the young person's hip new gadget, Blu Tack.

LOWEST MOMENT: Trying to strike a coconut with a giant pencil and failing horribly.

RELEVANT QUOTES: 'I'm sitting on two grand … in cash' – Lolly as she produces an envelope of money during the 'Most cash' prize task; 'Friendship is truth, truth is friendship' – Lolly attempting to explain the narrative behind her choreography to a ringtone

* On the main show. The youngest EVER contestant is the booze-swilling, cigarette-smoking Lenny Rush, who was fourteen years old at the time of his performance on New Year's Treat 2024.

FROM STAGE TO SCREEN Part 2

With our massive host, brilliant contestants and a magical director on board, we had what we thought was a solid team. But four years later, we were still being told that wasn't enough by the TV bigwigs. All the channels said it *sounded* fun, but surely comedians needed a script? Surely it'd be better if they knew the tasks they were being set in advance? And surely it'd be more fun if there were different comedians taking part each week?

Like honey-covered cowboys, we stuck to our guns. No, we said, comedians are funny people. They don't *always* need scripts. No, we said, the surprise when you open a task is the fundamental point of the idea. And no, we said, the rivalry of a returning cast is also a fundamental point of the idea, but arguably not quite as fundamental as the point about it being a surprise.

They listened. Channel 4 gave us some money to develop the idea. We developed the idea.

They said they still weren't sure.

Then another channel, Dave, saw something in us. Whether it was the vibrant shoots of a new, special telly flower, the undoubted appeal of Greg Davies or just the realisation that the only way to stop us pitching this idea was to give us a show, they green-lit our first six episodes.

Over a year later, the first episode went out to a definitely mixed reaction. But people soon got used to the cocktail of unplanned madness, free-wheeling comedians and a sitcom-style cast that developed its own story-lines as the series progressed. We made it to the end. Josh Widdicombe won a karate trophy because we weren't sure if we'd be back.

Dave had faith. They commissioned two more series. And then two more. Eventually, we'd make nine series for the brilliantly supportive channel before moving to our first investors, the mighty Channel 4 and, we hoped, a slightly larger terrestrial audience. This was the channel where I'd watched my comedy as a teenager and it felt like a dream home for us.

We've managed to make another nine series for Channel 4, the first three during the pandemic, and are still going today. I now have three children, and have had the undoubted honour of working closely and becoming friends with ninety comedians, and twenty unlikely celebrities for our New Year's Treat editions. The production team, led by Andy Cartwright and Vicky Winter, has swelled and stayed close, got married and had babies.

It really has been an absolute casserole of a decade.

EDINBURGH TASK 1
14 September 2009

Many thanks and congratulations. You have agreed to take part in the 2010 Edinburgh Challenge: an excellent decision.

A total of twenty eminent competitors are taking part this year.

I haven't quite decided when to let you know who you all are, but I'm almost certain I will at some point before the year is up.

Business time: There shall be twelve tasks set over the course of the next twelve months. The first is this:

MONEY FUN

Please deposit a sum of money into my Barclays bank account: number, sort code.

Whoever sends me the most money will receive 10 points, the second most 8 points, the third 6, fourth 4 and the fifth 2.

The person (or people) who sends me the least money will be docked 10 points.

The total amount I receive will make up the prize pot for the 2010 Edinburgh challenge.

You have until the end of the month to make the transfer. That is the first task.

Good luck and good bye.

Alex

2

HELL IS HERE

LIFE IN THE TASKMASTER STUDIO

The Taskmaster studio. A place where dreams are made (if your dreams involve covering Nick Mohammed in inflatable doughnuts). But how did this little slice of Pinewood get transformed into the intimidating high court of the Taskmaster's judgements? Who has thrived under the pressure of the studio and who has wilted? And is there really a plaque dedicated to where Jessica Knappett fell off the stage? (Spoiler: yes.) Read on to find out …

OUR PITCH TO THE CHANNEL

Five comedians, one Taskmaster – this is a seriously epic comedy game show.

Taskmaster is the ultimate competitive comedy game show; a funny, infectious and stringent test of five fine comic minds, created and developed live by comedian Alex Horne.

Each show will see five comedians compete in a series of tasks set by the all-powerful Taskmaster. Some tasks will be set in advance, allowing our comics time to plan ambitious/ridiculous responses to the challenges. Some tasks will take place on the spot, testing the comedians' ability to think on their hilarious feet. Other tasks will happen without the contestants knowing anything about them (e.g. which player will ask the Taskmaster why his arm is in a sling first?) – the Taskmaster is always in charge.

Three tasks per show will be recorded as VTs in advance, with three or four smaller tasks happening live in the studio. Each episode will see the Taskmaster (Greg Davies), his trusty assistant Alex and all five competitors meet in a specially designed location (complete with live studio audience) to see who wins the most tasks and hence who will win that week's show, the haul of prizes and the Taskmaster Cup.

2 / HELL IS HERE

What's unique about *Taskmaster* is that these comics haven't just turned up on the day to take part, they have been preparing for months and they really want to win. Comedians are competitive. And creative. And nasty. Rivalry will be encouraged, dodgy tactics rewarded and bribes accepted. This is the most cut-throat comedy show on TV.

The five comedians will remain the same throughout the series, building up a camaraderie and genuine sense of competition. However, each episode will be self-contained and standalone, so it's all to play for each week and a winner will be announced at the end of each show.

The Taskmaster and his assistant

Greg Davies is the Taskmaster. He will set the tasks and he will decide who wins. He can make up point systems and change the rules as the show goes along. He might be harsh, but he will always be fair.

Points will be handed out for success, ingenuity and wit. If the Taskmaster judges that someone has done something with style and aplomb, he may award them more points than someone who took the shortest route. The contestants will learn to please the Taskmaster – they will want to please the Taskmaster.

As Greg's right-hand man, Alex will dish out the sneakier details, adjudicate when facts and figures are involved, and generally do Greg's dirty work. He'll be on hand with statistics and graphics, he'll deliver the

Taskmaster's messages and he'll spy on the contestants' progress. On set he'll be positioned at his own desk, packed with technology, not unlike his role in BBC4's *We Need Answers*.

> This was the final version of the *Taskmaster* pitch that was presented to the first potential contestants in 2014 in a bid to persuade them to do the show. We had been fine-tuning the idea for four years before anyone agreed to make it and this turned out to be a fairly accurate representation of what the show would become. The main differences between reality and this document are:
>
> - We do not do tasks without the contestants knowing they are doing tasks. (We decided this would be too much like a prank show.)
> - We only do one task in the studio each episode.
> - Greg does not give out points for 'wit'.
> - I do not have my own desk.

GREG'S INTRODUCTIONS TO ALEX AT THE START OF EVERY SERIES

Series 1: As always, I am both aided and fluffed by my personal assistant, Alex Horne.

Series 2: I'm also joined once again by my lovely assistant, Mr Alex Horne.

Series 3: And here my faithful servant and would-be friend, Alex Horne.

Series 4: And for the fourth series in a row, I'm assisted and sat next to … Little Alex Horne.

Series 5: And here once more, desperately hoping for a better introduction than this, it's Little Alex Horne.

Series 6: And I'm afraid he's back again, it's my impersonal assistant, [singing] he says he's tall, but he's not tall, it's Little Alex Horne.

Series 7: And next to me, he looks after the facts and figures, but I have full control over his salary, he's little, he's Alex, he's Little Alex Horne.

Series 8: And here beside me, he's back, and he's no bigger than before, and I still find him utterly repugnant, it's Little Alex Horne.

Series 9: But now he's back, of course he's back, what else would he be doing, he's had literally no other offers, it's Little Alex Horne.

Series 10: And next to me, the man whose job it is to keep track of all the facts and figures, he's been my personal assistant for coming up to six years, and yet we have genuinely only socialised together three times. His neck is the same width as his head, he chooses to wear plastic slip-on shoes and he once told me, at some point nearly every day, he cries. It's Little Alex Horne.

Series 11: And next to me, a man who once told me that he's got no respect for the military, and if any soldier came up to him in public he could easily have them, because they're all stupid. It's Little Alex Horne.

Series 12: And now to my assistant. Usually I introduce him in a derogatory way, but for a change I thought he could read the introduction I've written for him. Over to you. [Alex] My name is Alex and in interviews I pretend Greg and I are friends in real life, but in truth we barely know each other. Also, I've got a little winkie. [Greg] It's Little Alex Horne.

Series 13: And next to me, the freshly thawed corpse of an ancient peat bog man. It's Little Alex Horne.

Series 14: And next to me, a man who recently confided to me when drunk that, before bed each night, his wife puts talcum powder on his rear end and special area, in what he described to me as his 'night night bot bot powder party'. It's Little Alex Horne.

Series 15: And now it's over to pricktionary corner. It's the direct result of a tryst between Postman Pat and Chewbacca … It's Little Alex Horne.

Series 16: We all know the following slogans: 'Just do it', 'Always the real thing', 'I'm loving it'. The most enduring brands all have one, so why shouldn't he? Please welcome, friendless oddball, Little Alex Horne.

Series 17: And sitting next to me is the Harry to my Megan Markle. A little ginger who's started to realise that he's paired up with one sassy queen. It's Little Alex Horne.

OUR PITCH TO THE CHANNEL Continued

The tasks

The challenges and competition will be taken seriously, but there will also be an underlying spirit of ridiculousness; tests will sometimes be utterly pointless and the challengers must carry out their tasks wholeheartedly, whatever the object.

There will be four types of task on the show – tasks on location, on-the-spot tasks (often shot at each competitor's home), studio tasks and secret tasks (played out live in the studio).

Tasks filmed on location will be filmed on VT and played into the room during the show (imagine beautifully shot VTs in the style of *The Apprentice*). Some tasks will involve each contestant presenting their VT individually, while others may involve a location shoot where all the contestants were involved simultaneously. When carrying out tasks individually, our competitors may not have any idea what their competitors have come up with until studio day, so the pressure is on to be ambitious and original.

The location

Set in a warehouse, club or reclaimed theatre, with a live audience, this show will look very different to your average studio panel show. With a feel similar to *Top Gear* or *Modern Life is Goodish*, *Taskmaster* is an event that happens in the real world, rather than a constructed television set. The space will really establish the tone of the show and set it apart from other comedy panel shows. This show was born as an Edinburgh show, and we want to maintain the heart and soul of the idea, with that feel of it being a real event that everyone is invested in, rather than a construct for the television.

Location suggestion: the Brixton Electric

Originally a cinema, the Brixton Electric has been through numerous incarnations and is now a highly adaptable space, with a real sense of atmosphere that will give the show a feeling of location and identity without the need for an elaborate set build.

During the show, the Taskmaster and his assistant will present each of the contestant's VTs to the players, and to the live audience. Between each VT there will be time for the Taskmaster and the other contestants to cross-examine each player on their efforts. Banter, bickering and bullshitting are what this show's all about.

> Apart from not going to the Brixton Electric, pretty much everything else here came true. Today, I hope, the show still feels like a real event that we are all invested in. Every series I am still excited to see how the new cast of five will tackle the tasks. And each year I'm surprised by the ingenuity and commitment of our contestants. It is, basically, my life now.

INTRODUCTION TO THE STUDIO

Setting tasks for the comedians in the first series of the TV show was the easy bit. Just as we still do today, I came up with a list of challenges, the Andys massaged that list into something televisually feasible but still funny, and we filmed the contestants in isolation at the same Taskmaster house that we've inhabited ever since.

I am often asked if we test the tasks before trying them in the show. We do make sure they work to some extent with members of the production team, some of their friends and some of my children, but one little known fact is that series 7 contestant Phil Wang was once our first guinea pig. A week before Christmas 2014, the erudite and physically memorable comedian was summoned to TM HQ and made to throw teabags, eat watermelon and phone a pizza company with strict limitations on his vocabulary.

To be honest, we didn't learn all that much from Phil, other than it looked like this was going to work. Comedians *are* funny people! They are also unpredictable. So most of the time we have to have faith that a task will work and the comedians will do the things in different ways from each other and from anything we might have anticipated. And so our first cast competed, sometimes exceptionally well, sometimes exceptionally badly, and we had our raw material.

The studio itself was unchartered territory. Unlike the Edinburgh show, this had to work. We had been granted a TV show, we had a proper host and an expectant audience. We also had five comedians who had put themselves through the wringer without really knowing why.

AN ABSOLUTE CASSEROLE

So with James Dillon, designer extraordinaire and the nicest of men, we talked for hours about the angles of the chairs, and how best our panel could be interrogated by Greg while also being able to see the footage we'd recorded and be seen by the gladiatorial audience. Thankfully, we landed on a site that would aid all these discussions thanks to its unique appearance and feel (including sticky walls and light up disco flooring).

The Clapham Grand in southwest London first opened in 1900 and has been a historic music hall venue, a classic bingo base and the sort of nightclub you remember fondly and with some shame for the rest of your life. Elephants stomped across its stage a hundred years ago, Charlie Chaplin performed there, as have Oasis, Public Enemy and now, Skinner, Widdicombe, Conaty, Ranganathan and Key. It is iconic.

We always wanted our audience to feel like they were witnessing a live event, rather than watching a chat. It should, we thought, be something of a bear pit where our contestants would have to scrap it out for the Taskmaster's approval points. At the Grand, the crowd surrounded the comics thanks to the layered seats and gaudy boxes, with the back wall and stage perfect for projection and live tasks. The lustrous red and gold columns were already there, as well as the overblown emblems and regal balconies. We just added the thrones and have kept the look ever since, even though we've moved around various TV studios, ending up at our long-term home, Pinewood Studios.

Like many aspects of the show, the studio element therefore seemed to click pretty much straightaway. It was just the right level of grandeur to juxtapose with the nonsense the comedians were made to do. *Taskmaster* is all about taking silly things seriously.

2 / HELL IS HERE

We did do one practice show there before recording series 1, a 'show zero' with our five inaugural contestants and tasks we didn't deem worthy of the actual series. In this historic and mainly unseen episode, Greg had a cane in the shape of a letter T which he would bash to underline his authority, as well as a slightly more pantomime-like demeanour.

For the real thing, we dialled this back a bit. It didn't quite seem fair on the contestants to *always* put them down. Occasionally they'd done something well and we realised quickly that the Taskmaster needed to be reasonably fair, despite the dictatorial set up. So we lost the stick, relaxed into our roles and recorded the first ever series of *Taskmaster*.

STUDIO FACTS

🦆 Most successful live tasker ever: Dara Ó Briain (six solo wins, average points scored in live tasks 4.30)

🦆 Least successful live tasker ever: Sian Gibson (one solo win, average points scored in live tasks 1.40)

THE STAGE

Location of all live studio tasks – with remnants of paint, egg and the last of Ed Gamble's patience with David Baddiel to prove it.

STAGE RIGHT
The site where James Acaster tragically lost a hula tournament to Phil Wang.

CENTRE STAGE
The Miracle of Toilet Paper Tower, where Sophie Duker stood her ground against Chris Ramsey's shoe.

STAGE LEFT
The raging hippo of Daisy May Cooper, who could not get a cowering Richard Herring to guess what her drawing looked like.

THE KNAPPETT
The site of great devastation, where Jessica Knappett fell from the stage while doing a silly walk. This part of the stage has been known as the Knappett ever since.

THE SEATS
Location of the studio chat – may still contain the tears of Joe Wilkinson.

2 / HELL IS HERE

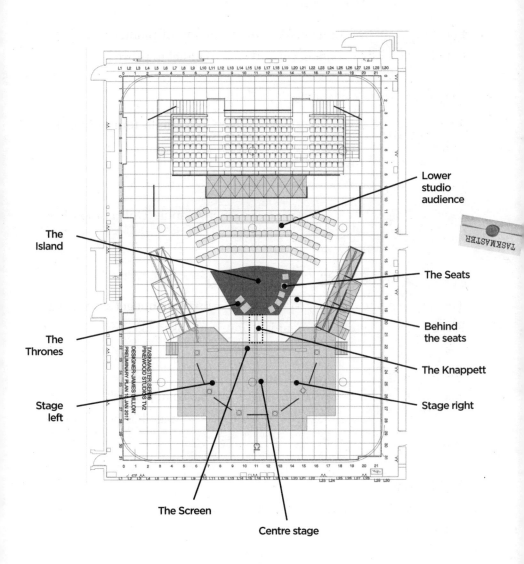

BEHIND THE SEATS

Greg's naughty corner, where he takes contestants who have not put the effort in and/or called him a pussy for failing to open a box.

THE THRONES
- The mighty throne of Greg Davies
- The less mighty throne of Alex Horne (no arm rests).

THE ISLAND

Various sites of importance:
- Where Joe Wilkinson did make himself prostrate and beg forgiveness from Greg for his terrible cheating
- Where Bridget Christie did lure Greg into an ancient dance while yelling the word 'stopcock'
- Where John Robins did encourage the entire cast to do a little jump
- Where Sophie Willan did do a slutdrop and it was great (still only got 2 points).

THE STUDIO AUDIENCE

Possible vicinity of Rhod Gilbert's inflatable doughnut.

Seat of the only person other than Greg to decide a tiebreaker (series 5, episode 6).

TAKING TIME

Some tasks on *Taskmaster* are about speed and efficiency. And some are about a former doctor spending most of the day trying to fart in an airplane. Here are the tasks that took the longest time.

Longest task involving EVERY contestant

TASK: Grow the longest nail

TIMEFRAME: Ten weeks

EPISODE: Series 1, episode 5 ('Little Denim Shorts')

WINNER: Josh Widdicombe (2.8cm, thumbnail) – accurately described as 'the worst thing you're ever going to see'

OTHER NOTABLE ATTEMPTS: Tim Key claimed he was exempt because he was performing in a play at the time, as a character who bit his nails. He went so far as to get a letter from the producer excusing him from the task. Rightfully last place.

RELEVANT QUOTE: 'Oh my god, it's curled over. Why has it curled over?' – Roisin Conaty on Romesh Ranganathan's attempt (2.2cm, fingernail)

Longest task involving ANY contestant

3rd place

TASK: Keep the basketball on the running machine for as long as possible

TIMEFRAME: Four months – the basketball stayed on the treadmill outside the Taskmaster house until Storm Doris blew it off

EPISODE: Series 4, episode 2 ('Look At Me')

CONTESTANT: Hugh Dennis

METHODOLOGY: Hugh held the ball down with a plastic tub so that it stayed on the running machine, before getting Alex to bring him the power plug that the machine was connected to and unplugging the machine.

SCORE: 5 points

OTHER NOTABLE ATTEMPTS: Noel Fielding attempted to use sofa cushions, which worked for 3.75 seconds – approximately 2,803,507 times shorter than Hugh managed.

RELEVANT QUOTE: 'It's quite boring, isn't it? You don't think you might just get me a book?' – Hugh Dennis, midway through his record-breaking task attempt

2nd place

TASK: Send a cheeky anonymous text to the Taskmaster every day

TIMEFRAME: Five months

EPISODE: Series 5, episode 5 ('A Wind Dried Puffin')

CONTESTANT: Mark Watson

2 / HELL IS HERE

FIRST TEXT SENT: 'Hey, sexy, just getting in touch. This is the first of 150 messages. You're in for a treat.'

TWELFTH TEXT SENT: 'I have a big dick.'

SCORE: 0 – Watson was supposed to send 150 texts, but he sent just 148, so Greg, who genuinely received all of these anonymous texts, disqualified him: 'Five months of irritation bubbling up here.'

RELEVANT QUOTE: 'What a terrible waste of time.' – Greg Davies

'I'm shattered to get no points out of something which, genuinely, if I look back on this calendar year, it's one of the major things I've done with it.' – Mark Watson

1st place

TASK: Make a photo portfolio of the golden pineapple with other esteemed company

TIMEFRAME: Six months

EPISODE: Series 5, episode 6 ('Spoony Neeson')

CONTESTANT: Aisling Bea

WHAT HAPPENED: Aisling sent the golden pineapple to her mother in Ireland, who spent six months diligently taking photos of it around notable hotspots (a blacksmiths, a church, a stable).

SCORE: 0 – but a deserved round of applause for Aisling's mum

RELEVANT QUOTE: 'If a boyfriend of mine passes three months and makes it to Ireland, my mother brings him back and puts him on one of those simulator horses to see how fast he can go.' – Aisling, on the esteemed jockey simulator in Kildare

PRIZE TASK WINS

Every episode starts with the prize task, where contestants bring in items for the episode winner to take home. (NB: These are not gifts for Greg, despite what Sophie Willan believes.) And every contestant has a different approach to this task: you can do a Mark Watson and spend lots of money and time crafting the perfect prize, or you can take the Daisy May Cooper approach and pick up the first thing you see on your way to the studio (and earn pretty much as many points as Mark). However, some contestants have a gift for prizes. Here are the most successful prize taskers of all time.

Mawaan Rizwan

NUMBER OF PRIZE TASK WINS: 5

SERIES: 10

SERIES POINTS: 151 (2.96 points per task)

POSITION IN SERIES: Third, thanks mostly to these prize tasks

BEST PRIZE TASKS: A full-size microphone costume for 'best thing that's bigger at the top than the bottom'; a shrine to himself made when he was 16 for 'most narcissistic thing'; lentils and rice in a Tupperware container that he stole from his housemate for 'cheekiest thing'.

RELEVANT QUOTE: 'I'll be honest, the audience reaction … it deserved better.' – Mawaan, on his microphone costume

2 / HELL IS HERE

Desiree Burch

NUMBER OF PRIZE TASK WINS: 5

SERIES: 12

SERIES POINTS: 161 (3.22 points per task)

POSITION IN SERIES: Third, alongside Alan Davies

BEST PRIZE TASKS: Using chicken cutlets to represent boobs in the 'thing that, if you put it in a bag and sit on it, it would feel the nicest'; a chaise longue in the 'most old fashioned thing that you still use'; an obsolete integrated cat latrine that she now has to use as a very expensive cupboard in the 'best thing you use for something other than its actual purpose' task.

RELEVANT QUOTE: 'Just give her the five points now.' – Guz Khan, on Desiree's prize task entry of a specially commissioned picture of a dog wearing one of Guz's coats

Ardal O'Hanlon

NUMBER OF PRIZE TASK WINS: 5

SERIES: 13

SERIES POINTS: 153 (3.06 points per task)

POSITION IN SERIES: Fourth

BEST PRIZE TASKS: A mirror, in the 'object you would most like to show to an alien' task; night vision goggles (lights and swimming goggles) in the 'best night time thing' task; a tea towel (which he would use to cover his face to make a baby laugh) in the 'most calming item' task.

RELEVANT QUOTE: 'I should point out he's not a real doctor, he's more of a life coach.' – Ardal, explaining why a finger puppet named Dr Jerry Flynn was his entry for the 'nicest thing to put your finger in' task.

HONOURABLE MENTION

Steve Pemberton (series 17), who 'only' managed four prize task wins in series 17, brought in some of the most remarkable prize tasks ever. These including a giant papier mâché moon featuring dozens of pictures of Alex Horne's bare bottom, a haiku about the Taskmaster written entirely on a calculator and, arguably the greatest prize task ever, a cryptic crossword that he had written and had been published in the *Guardian* on the day of the recording with the hidden message 'Greg, please give Steve all five points.'

TASKMASTER HALL OF GLORY
Oldest Contestant

NAME: Julian Clary

AGE AT EPISODE TRANSMISSION: A spry 65 years

SERIES: 16

POINTS: 155 (3.10 points per task)

POSITION IN SERIES: Second and one good throw of a ball into a bath away from being first

FUN FACT: Julian Clary was the first contestant to bring a friend's ashes in as a prize. Is that fun?*

GREATEST ACHIEVEMENT: Being the quickest to pull the sword from the stone when the password was 'Josh Widdicombe', despite the fact that he couldn't remember Josh Widdicombe's name and referred to him instead as 'the small and nasally one'.

LOWEST MOMENT: Being chased by rubbish robots and lasting just three seconds (as one rammed into him almost immediately).

RELEVANT QUOTE: 'What sort of people enjoy this programme? Is it students?'

* Thankfully, as Julian won the episode, he was allowed to take his friends' ashes home at the end of the show.

Edinburgh Task 1: How Did It Go?

In the end, 18 comedians sent money to my bank account, with amounts ranging from 13p (the Sweden-based Al Pitcher) to Mark Watson's winning £104 sum. Other highlights, setting the scene for the entire year, were Mike Wozniak's £1 Jersey note, the second place £102.34 from Lloyd Langford (star of *Taskmaster Australia* season 2) and Tim Key, who paid *minus* £40, in the form of an invoice, which meant I had to pay him.

EDINBURGH TASK 2
1 October 2009

Hello there.

So, task 1 is now over. There are a couple of payments still to be cleared, but thank you. Remarkable stuff.

There is still some totting up to be done, but you may be interested to hear that the prize pot will definitely stand somewhere between £250 and £1,000. That's right. Considerable. The first task also produced plenty of fighting talk: 'I'm going to win this thing' — that sort of carry on.

So now we know how much is at stake, let's get down to the serious business of the second task:

FIND A HEDGEHOG

You must find a hedgehog.

You must then let me know that you have found a hedgehog.

How you do this is up to you, but you must convince me that you have found a hedgehog.

If I am convinced that you have found a hedgehog you shall receive 10 points.

If I am not convinced that you have found a hedgehog you shall receive 0 points.

You have one month to find a hedgehog.

Good luck and good bye.

Alex

3

LITTLE POLYTHENE GRIEF CAGE

A GUIDE TO THE TASKMASTER HOUSE

What would *Taskmaster* be without the Taskmaster house? It would be a bunch of comedians debasing themselves in an empty lot next to a golf course. You'd probably still watch it, but something would be missing (like a roof or a kitchen for making ravioli stuffed with dog food). Welcome to the Taskmaster headquarters. Don your gold shoes, give the Taskmaster portrait a smack on the lips and head inside.

HOUSE QUEENS REAL ESTATE
CHECK OUT THIS CHARMING LONDON PROPERTY, FULL OF CHARACTER AND PERFECT FOR FAMILIES.

CHISWICK'S NO.1 ESTATE AGENT

Beautiful cottage property in the Chiswick W4 area, complete with static caravan, music hutch, shed and biodome/dream orb/transparent boutique/hip-hop hideout. Secret cake room and Linda the Cow not included. Close to golf course for annoying golfers with whistles and/or chasing balloons.

NB: Planning permission for an extension was granted in 2018, but a fallout between the builders Acaster, Gilbert, Wang and Co. meant it was never completed.

3 / LITTLE POLYTHENE GRIEF CAGE

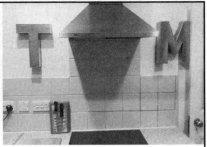

ENTRANCE HALL
- Complete with five traditional pigeon-holes (seventeen previous owners)
- Large portrait of popular comedian Greg Davies (kissed many times by Joe Lycett)
- Chic doorbell (may contain the blood of Richard Herring)
- Door and surrounding walls slightly damaged by Claudia Winkleman and her massive pole
- Front door spacious enough to hide one Hugh Dennis

BATHROOM
- Cosy bathroom containing loo roll holder (some surface damage courtesy of Lee Mack)
- Sizeable toilet seat (fits at least one loo roll tube through it, as verified by Iain Stirling)
- Pictures of mice and fish from the hobby of previous tenant (Australian)

KITCHEN
- Kitchen space sufficient to cook pancakes, dog food pasta and surprisingly pleasant fish sausages
- Kitchen sink with beautiful water feature designed by Jo Brand (may contain remnants of Kiell Smith-Bynoe's imaginary friend)
- Cooking amenities: oven (may contain remnants of Frankie Boyle's imaginary friend), blender (not functioning due to camel mishap) and microwave (butter not included)
- Washing machine (slight damage from cake)

RECEPTION ROOM
- Flexible decor allowing for constant refreshing
- Sofa tall enough to hide one Lucy Beaumont
- French doors to garden, perfect for throwing coconuts through
- Plenty of storage space in the form of secret doors and cupboards in the walls (mostly filled with plastic bricks and balls of string)
- Ornate table (underside may conceal secret messages to Sarah Millican)

SHOWER ROOM
- Snug shower room (may contain one Lolly Adefope hiding behind a plank)

LABORATORY
- Beautiful windowless laboratory, perfect for hosting melon buffets and building lemon towers
- Decorated with remnants of old meals (toothpaste pie, wasabi jelly babies, Marmite and porridge ice cream)
- NB: Unpleasant smell due to a woman from South Shields pouring milk on the floor. We're looking into it.

3 / LITTLE POLYTHENE GRIEF CAGE

GARDEN
- Stunning garden space, includes beheaded duck in a shallow grave dug by Ed Gamble
- Potential to become a go-kart track as used by Jess Knappett in a plumber's outfit
- Nearby road access for cars/giant gong deliveries
- Stage area perfect for balancing a ladder on your chin, holding your breath whilst handcuffed in a bath, or spanking yourself with a wooden spoon
- Tall trees (may contain Patatas the cat)

GROUND FLOOR
1,009 square feet/93.75 square metres

THE CARAVAN

Step into luxury with the static caravan of your dreams! With its stylish faded brown cushions and distinctive fragrance, it's sure to make you say, 'It's actually not a bad caravan' (Jamali Maddix, series 11).

Fancy yourself an artist? This caravan doubles up as an artist's studio if you're Katy Wix and like drawing pictures of Frida Kahlo on your elbow, or if you're Mel Giedroyc and fancy drawing a portrait of a woman behind a curtain. Or maybe you crave EXCITEMENT and DANGER, in which case you can turn this caravan into an escape room for people who are really hungry for grapes. Or, if you're Lou Sanders, pop some tremendous legs on the top, tape some fireworks to the bottom of them and turn the roof into a roller disco!

3 / LITTLE POLYTHENE GRIEF CAGE

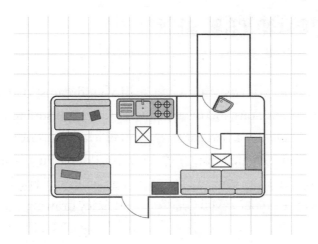

Vital statistics

- Surprisingly spacious (with secret cake room/dressing up area at the back)
- Circumference measures 400 baked beans (as measured by Phil Wang)
- Circumference measures 2,550 baked beans (as measured by Rhod Gilbert)
- Contains dress-up room, sink and the ghost of a young woman that only Lee Mack can conjure
- Table damaged by a very scary man named Butch
- Superficial damage to door caused by paint bottle exploded by Jamali Maddix's foot
- Hole-in-wall feature created by Rhod Gilbert's javelin
- Floor may contain blood of Aisling Bea
- Roof access possible (complete with clock)
- Outside decorated with TV ariel/tiny ladder (if you're John Kearns).

STUFF IN THE SHED
(AKA recycled props)

Sometimes props from one task turn up in another. Some people would say this reflects the Taskmaster's ceaseless dedication to recycling and producing a sustainable show. Others would say it's a natural consequence of having a shed where you can bung any old junk. Here are all the times props have been reused in the show.

1. Grape scissors

WHAT ARE THEY: Scissors for cutting grapes

BROUGHT IN BY: Frank Skinner, series 1, episode 1, for 'Most unusual item' (4 points)

USED AGAIN BY: Production team during series 14, episode 10, as a way to help contestants cut the grapes once they had escaped the caravan in the 'Eat the grape' task 2.

2. The Orgasmatron

WHAT IS IT: An effective head massager with a filthy name

BROUGHT IN BY: Roisin Conaty, series 1, episode 6, for 'Most satisfying item' (1 point)

USED AGAIN BY: Alex Horne on various contestants on the New Year's Treat 2023 during the 'Recreate the picture from a massage chair' task. It was particularly successful on British Olympic hero Sir Mo Farah. Alex gave the gold-medal winning athlete a head massage and Sir Mo started giggling uncontrollably.

3. Xylophone

WHAT IS IT: A child's colourful musical instrument

REQUESTED BY: Frank Skinner and Romesh Ranganathan, series 1, episode 6, as one of the ingredients in their 'alphabet meal'

USED AGAIN BY: Production team during series 11, episode 7, as part of one of the many mini-tasks contestants had to complete after Alex had set fire to the main task.

THEN USED AGAIN BY: Production team during series 17, episode 4, when contestants had to work out who they were shaking hands with – the fourth hand was filled with the xylophone (as the answers spelled out 'ALEX HORNE').

4. Cricket bat

WHAT IS IT: A bat for playing cricket

BROUGHT IN BY: Doc Brown, in the 'Buy the Taskmaster a gift' task in series 2, episode 3, as part of a set, along with a helmet – Greg and his sister would play a game called Mad Helmet Murderer, where he would hit his (helmet-wearing) sister in the head with a cricket bat. (3 points)

USED AGAIN BY: Paul Chowdhry as a way of propelling his pea in series 3, episode 1 (unsuccessfully).

THEN USED AGAIN BY: Al Murray in the 'Pop the balloons' task, series 3, episode 2 (unsuccessfully).

5. Googly eyes

WHAT ARE THEY: Cartoonish eyes that can be stuck on any item to make it look sentient

BROUGHT IN BY: Noel Fielding, series 4, episode 5, for 'Cutest thing' (5 points)

USED AGAIN BY: Production team during series 16, episode 5, for the 'Make the most cool but scary gang using these eyes' task.

THEN USED AGAIN BY: Joanne McNally during the 'Make this mannequin come alive' task in series 17, episode 8 – it had googly eyes while she performed CPR on it (unsuccessfully).

6. Air horn

WHAT IS IT: A very, very, very loud horn that Jessica Knappett can impersonate perfectly

BROUGHT IN BY: Aisling Bea, series 5, episode 1, for 'Most excellent noise' (3 points)

USED AGAIN BY: Production team as part of many items on offer to contestants in the 'Guess what a contestant will do with these items' task, Series 7, episode 2.

7. Sausage presentation unit

WHAT IS IT: A wind-up toy elephant with a fork on the end, presenting a sausage to the world

BROUGHT IN BY: Bob Mortimer, series 5, episode 6, in the 'Best homemade item' task (5 obviously deserved points)

USED AGAIN BY: Bob Mortimer, Champion of Champions 1, episode 2, in the 'Best thing' task – but modified this time to be a broccoli rotation and delivery unit (just 3 points – outrageous).

8. Propeller hat

WHAT IS IT: A hat with a propeller on it

BROUGHT IN BY: Production team, as part of the 'Best quick-change outfit' task, series 7, episode 1

USED AGAIN BY: Sophie Duker, as the hat she chose in the 'Throw a hat on the Taskmaster' task in Champion of Champions 3 (3 points).

THEN USED AGAIN BY: Joanne McNally, again in the 'Make this mannequin come alive' task – as well as big googly eyes it had on this propeller hat, neither of which helped when it was declared dead at the scene by Joanne (1 point).

9. Knitted series 7 cast in birdcage

WHAT IS IT: The cast of series 7 (James Acaster, Jessica Knappett, Kerry Godliman, Phil Wang and Rhod Gilbert) in their *Taskmaster* outfits in knitted form (not actual size)

CREATED BY: The partner of one of the production team, who completed them extremely late at night on a school night

USED BY: Johnny Vegas in the 'Convince a security guard to look in your bag' task, series 10, episode 4. He used reverse psychology and his own unhinged demeanour to tempt the security guard into looking into the bag (which contained the unlucky knitted series 7 cast members).

10. Greedy Esquire

WHAT IS IT: A homemade sewn version of the Mr Men character Mr Greedy that turned out to be so elegant it had to be renamed Greedy Esquire (also called a one-eyed testicle by Greg)

BROUGHT IN BY: Victoria Coren Mitchell, series 12, episode 5, 'Most elegant thing beginning with G' (2 points)

USED AGAIN BY: Victoria Coren Mitchell, series 12, episode 7, 'Most ridiculous thing', where she used Greg's ridiculing of Greedy Esquire in the previous episode to successfully argue that she should get five points here.

11. 'Wayne' the air dancer

WHAT IS IT: One of those tubes filled with air that dances, usually outside car washes, invented for the 1996 Atlanta Olympic Games (fun fact)

3 / LITTLE POLYTHENE GRIEF CAGE

BROUGHT IN BY: Desiree Burch, series 12, episode 10, 'Most magnificent floppy thing' (5 points)

USED AGAIN BY: Production team for series 16, episode 7, where contestants had to pie 'Wayne' in the face and if they missed they had to mirror his dancing for ten seconds. This particularly infuriated Sue Perkins, who hated Wayne with a passion.

12. The wind-powered owl

WHAT IS IT: A wind-powered owl with a bobbing head

BROUGHT IN BY: Ardal O'Hanlon for the 'Get the most surprising thing delivered to the Taskmaster house' task – it was decreed not that exciting by Greg (2 points)

USED AGAIN BY: Julian Clary and Sam Campbell in series 16, episode 6 when reenacting Lucy Beaumont's garage scene, as a substitute for a flamingo.

THEN USED AGAIN BY: Steve Pemberton in the 'Flick, flip and flap a flip flop, flan and flapjack' task, to add extra flappiness to his flapping a flapjack flattempt.

13. The alluring tiger

WHAT IS IT: A cuddly Bengal tiger

BROUGHT IN BY: Production team as part of the 'Pin an alluring tail on the alluring animal while blindfolded' task in series 14, episode 8

USED AGAIN BY: Steve Pemberton in the 'Be the most impressive load-bearer' task, as one of the many items he balanced on his back while waving.

14. The ahoy hat

WHAT IS IT: A sailor's hat that will delight and entertain your fellow drivers on a long car journey

BROUGHT IN BY: John Kearns, series 14, episode 7, for 'The thing you'd most like to have with you on a car journey' (2 points, harsh)

USED AGAIN BY: Alex Horne (and every contestant in series 15) as the hat to wear while driving the barge in series 15, episode 1 – Alex called it a 'safety hat', although it didn't protect him when the barge crashed during Jenny's attempt.

15. The Black Death doctor outfit

WHAT IS IT: An outfit worn by doctors during the Black Death with a long pointy nose

BROUGHT IN BY: Dara Ó Briain for 'Best fancy dress', series 14, episode 8 (3 points)

USED AGAIN BY: Production team as one of the many outfits Lucy Beaumont and Sue Perkins had to wear (and not tell the other contestants they were putting on) during the 'Recreate your team-mate's garage scene' task in series 16, episode 6.

16. Dog mask

WHAT IS IT: A latex dog mask of an Alsatian, with quite alarming eyes and a lolling tongue

BROUGHT IN BY: Jenny Eclair for the 'Sneakiest thing' task, as she hid her YA novel behind the mask as an attempt to publicise it (4 points)

USED AGAIN BY: Sophie Willan in the 'Make this mannequin come alive' task, as the head of her character 'Wolfie' (she was a Scorpio,

3 / LITTLE POLYTHENE GRIEF CAGE

36, looking for love, who had the hidden 'talents' of dancing and beatboxing).

THEN USED AGAIN BY: The production team: Wolfie turned up again in series 17, episode 10, as the special friend that Sophie had to hug in the task 'Hug your special friend'.

17. The coward's glasses

WHAT ARE THEY: A pair of glasses with photos of Mae Martin's eyes in them so the user can hide when they are closing their eyes out of fear

BROUGHT IN BY: Mae Martin, for the 'Most heroic thing' task, series 15, episode 3 (It gained them 2 points, beating only a shower curtain with Enrique Iglesias' face on it.)

USED AGAIN BY: Lucy Beaumont in her disturbing (and powerful) piece 'Heads, shoulders, knees and toes' in series 16, episode 6. She wore the glasses while Alex wore a latex duck mask and slept on the couch. It ended with Lucy biting Alex's foot. It was genuinely quite upsetting.

18. The Greg puppet

WHAT IS IT: A wonderfully detailed wooden puppet of Greg Davies with working mouth and eyes, created by Mae Martin's father during lockdown (incredibly, a self-taught puppet-maker)

BROUGHT IN BY: Mae Martin, for the 'Best Greg Davies merchandise', in series 15, episode 10 (5 points)

USED AGAIN BY: The production team, who let him pop up in the bits before tasks in series 16.

BURNING DOWN (OR NEAR) THE HOUSE

For a show that is so dedicated to health and safety, a surprising number of people have been allowed to start fires in or near the Taskmaster house. It's getting to the stage where you have to suspect Alex Horne has a particularly lucrative fire insurance policy (one that pays out in the event of Lucy Beaumont burning down your house while trying to make some surprisingly pleasant sausages). Here's a list of every time flames have been used to fire contestants to glory.

1. Joe Lycett popped a bunch of fireworks in a cake and set them off, before licking some icing and wincing (series 4, episode 1).

2. Aisling Bea, Bob Mortimer, Mark Watson, Nish Kumar and Sally Phillips tried to light a candle in the caravan using a flame given to them in the lab. At one point Nish shouted 'YOU BUBBLY F***' so loudly that the candle went out (series 5, episode 6).

3. Asim Chaudhry made his little wind-up man's adventure through the underground in the garden more extraordinary by adding a mini flamethrower (series 6, episode 2).

4. James Acaster used fireworks (and Richard Osman) to deliver a task to Alex in the most spectacular way (series 7, episode 5).*

---

* In one of many favouritism scandals in series 7, Kerry Godliman claimed she wasn't allowed fireworks and James was. Alex revealed it was because she asked for the fireworks near the end of her task, when things weren't going too well, while James asked for the fireworks right away. So if you're going to use fire, make sure you do it immediately.

3 / LITTLE POLYTHENE GRIEF CAGE

5 In a task where the contestants had to poke the most unexpected thing through the hole of a grotto, Jessica Knappett waved a lit branch through (with Alex murmuring 'Just don't set fire to the tree' as she did so) (series 7, episode 8).

6 Sian Gibson set fire to her volcano to make it more exciting – claiming it was a 'party volcano' – and only received 2 points (series 8, episode 3).

7 Sian Gibson used fire again when she tried to set an eraser alight in an attempt to erase it completely. She abandoned this and then threw it in a hedge (series 8, episode 10).

8 Lou Sanders attached rockets to a pair of tremendous legs in some roller-skates and set them on fire, sending them very, very slowly across the caravan roof (series 8, episode 10).

9 David Baddiel set fire to *Taskmaster*'s Broadcast award and then tried to smash it with a hammer (series 9, episode 3).

10 Jamali Maddix got a blowtorch and set part of the wall on fire while vandalising it in the most creative way (before getting a cricket ball in the crotch from Charlotte Ritchie, who declared it 'epic') (series 11, episode 6).

11 Charlotte Ritchie, Jamali Maddix, Lee Mack, Mike Wozniak and Sarah Kendall had to complete as many tasks as possible after the task they were reading was set on fire in front of them. Mike Wozniak said a vole had no chutzpah (series 11, episode 7).

12 Jamali Maddix set fire to the sea when making extreme weather for Taskmaster Island (series 11, episode 9).

13 Sarah Millican created fire in her hands for her most spectacular catch (using forced perspective to make the fire in the distance look like it was in her hands). It was only slightly ruined by Alex using a fire extinguisher to put it out (series 14, episode 3).

14 Jenny Eclair achieved the 'Most impressive effect with a single breath' by setting the caravan curtains on fire and then immediately blowing them out, much to the relief of around a dozen fire officers who were required to attend (series 15, episode 2).

15 Julian Clary and Susan Wokoma had to deal with a fire taking place in the lobby of the Taskmaster Hotel (Julian Clary was particularly upset, murmuring, 'Oh no, a fire? How awful') (series 16, episode 10).

16 John Robins started a fire in a bucket and shot himself out of a cannon to create the best midair photograph (series 17, episode 5).

HONOURABLE MENTION

Krishnan Guru-Murthy set fire to a tower he was building in an attempt to make it lighter, forgetting that setting fire to something tends to destroy it. Krishnan is one of Britain's most respected journalists (New Year's Treat 1).

THE TASKMASTER DAY

The Taskmaster house is constantly occupied. Two-thirds of the time is spent preparing tasks, organising comedians' diaries and mopping up milk. The rest is spent doing, filming and observing the tasks themselves. Here is how a day in that part of *Taskmaster* life breaks down.

7am The first member of the team arrives. The oven is turned on, water boiled and radiators checked. It's often cold and the heating doesn't always work. Sometimes it's warm and on those days the heating often can't be turned off.

7.30am The camera department arrives. Without these people, *Taskmaster* is just desperate comedians doing pointless activities in a bungalow that is either too hot or too cold. So, no one questions what these people do for the next hour. It looks important and seems to involve taking apart every piece of their equipment, shaking their heads and then putting it all back together.

8am The contestant arrives. They are guided swiftly into their modest dressing room and offered toast and apologies. They are only allowed out if they ask permission, just in case they see anything that might hint at what's about to happen. Apprehensively they nibble breakfast and don whatever clothing they have chosen to wear for the experience.

8.10am The Taskmaster's assistant arrives. He asks if he's got there before the contestant and is let down gently. He also puts on his task clothing, usually in the freezing lab – he can put on an entire suit in under a minute – drinks a pint of liquified fruit and vegetables, and is ready by 8.15am.

For the next hour, the team, led by Andy D (which stands for 'Director'), agrees upon the order of tasks and makes sure each one is ready to be launched. Andy C (which stands for 'Courteous') opens the spreadsheets, the sound department fiddles with shirts; we are ready.

9.30am The contestant opens the first task of the day. These vary in length between five minutes and an hour. Seldom are they interrupted (if so, it's usually due to rain, planes or an unexpected delivery from Amazon) and if they are it is only briefly. They are over and done with quickly, and the contestant doesn't need to think about the task again until they are back in the studio. Often, however, they do. They stew over their decisions either until the next task or for the coming nights, turning over their decisions with disbelief until they are allowed to actually talk about them openly. For while in the *Taskmaster* world, you may never discuss the tasks themselves. Until you are in the presence of the Taskmaster.

11am In between their second, third or fourth task, the contestant decides what everyone has for lunch. This is an important moment: too stodgy and the afternoon becomes tricky; too healthy and the morning lacks enthusiasm.

1pm The food arrives, and every single person sits in a circle and eats whatever was chosen, and tells the contestant that they made a great choice.

2pm Four or five more tasks in the afternoon. It's important to keep them coming, not only so they all get done, but also to drive the

3 / LITTLE POLYTHENE GRIEF CAGE

contestant into a state of zen-like exhaustion; to drill down to the essence of the person; to strip them of their constructed comedic sensibilities; and expose the actual human underneath.

6pm They are released. Some have other commitments they must fulfil that evening – stand up, acting, socializing – but a much better option is to rent a yurt with a hot tub, and to just sit and stare until sleep.

7.30pm The member of the team who arrived first is also the last to leave. The camera department has taken apart their equipment and put it back together one more time. Vicky (production mother) has ensured that everyone has eaten enough and all the milk has been mopped up again. Everyone heads off to their other lives to do their own tasks in their own way. The doors are locked and the Taskmaster house rests.

TASKMASTER HALL OF GLORY
Most Inconsistent Contestant

NAME: Bridget Christie

NUMBER OF NON-TEAM TASKS SHE WON: 14

NUMBER OF NON-TEAM TASKS SHE CAME LAST IN: 15

SERIES: 13

POINTS: 157 (3.14 points per task)

POSITION IN SERIES: Third, having led for three episodes

FUN FACT: As revealed in the *Taskmaster Podcast*, Bridget's outfit was based on Lee Van Cleef's uniform in *The Good, The Bad and the Ugly*.

GREATEST ACHIEVEMENTS: Creating a genuinely moving tribute to the Soviet doggy cosmonaut, Laika, with a couple of traffic cones; making the longest shoes and biggest hat in the history of the show; recreating a remarkable rope-climbing photo.

LOWEST MOMENTS: Having a breakdown in the garden while banging a bunch of pots and pans; taking so long to find a shoe in a task that Alex got genuinely annoyed for the first time in thirteen series; ballsing up the 'Cup snake' task and having to use a very big log instead of cups.

RELEVANT QUOTE: 'Stopcock. Stopcock. Stopcock. STOPCOCK.'

Edinburgh Task 2: How Did It Go?

Tim Key retained the upper hand within our relationship by emailing me within six minutes ('Found one'). I had to take his word for it, because I'm not Greg Davies and he won the 10 points (in that first version of *Taskmaster* it was 10 points for the win, 9 points for second, 8 for third and so on). When I asked Tim later where and how he found the hedgehog, he tapped his nose and shook his head. Then he tapped my nose and shook my head.

The rest of the contestants struggled for months to lay eyes on the prickly mammals, with many resorting to trips to places like Tiggywinkles Wildlife Hospital in a desperate bid for points. Even this early in the competition anger was evident in terse excuse-filled emails from Messrs Edwards, Basden and Olver, while Mark Watson claimed that hedgehogs were actually mythical creatures.

EDINBURGH TASK 3
2 November 2009

Here we are again.

Quick update: some of you were pleased you have more time to find hedgehogs; some of you were angry. All emotions encouraged. Good stuff.

For now(ember), two quick tasks:

Number one:

NAME YOUR RIVALS

There are twenty of you. Send me the names of the twenty people you think I've asked to take part in this challenge.

That's it.

A point will be awarded for each correct guess.

Points will also be awarded to those ten people whose names are guessed the fewest times (10 to the least expected, 9 to the second least, etc etc). So it's not in your interest to go blabbing in your quest to seek these names. Deny it for now. Good.

In December I will reveal the correct twenty names. Indeed I will present them in the form of a league table. That's right. Naming and shaming time. Happy Christmas!

3 / LITTLE POLYTHENE GRIEF CAGE

Number two:

HERE COMES THE SUN

Send me one headline that you think will be on the front page of the *Sun* in January. Yes, it's a little while off, but December will be full of *The X Factor*. January will be in 2010. That's the future. Points will be awarded for accuracy (and, maybe, other stuff). So it's a *Sun* headline I want. Feel free to furnish me with any further details if you think you know what's round the corner.

So, send me twenty names and one headline. Entries must arrive by the end of this month. No exceptions.

Thank you.

Good luck.

Horne

PS For those of you contemplating bribery for points, why not? Give me something nice, I'll give you something nice. Blackmail, on the other hand, is less welcome.

4

THE ALPINE DARLING

TASKMASTER AND THE REST OF THE WORLD

It might seem implausible, but there is actually a world outside *Taskmaster* and it's one that occasionally impacts on the show. There have been contestants from all over the world – and possibly a few from outside the world as well (looking at no one, Bridget Christie). It's time for a whistlestop tour of places in the world in *Taskmaster*, so get your pencils out of your desk, do your best Hugh Dennis impression and get ready to learn some GEOGRAPHY.

LEAVING THE CONFINES

Every contestant has different thresholds of adventurousness. Some don't like to leave the house and some don't like to leave the room they're in (looking at you, Katherine Parkinson). But some view the big gates of the Taskmaster compound and yearn for freedom. This section is dedicated to those pioneers who dared to leave the estate and how far they actually got.

DISTANCE FROM HOUSE: 10 metres

EPISODE: Series 4, episode 8 ('Tony Three Pies')

CONTESTANT: Mel Giedroyc

TASK: Do the most surprising thing with this rubber duck

WHAT HAPPENED: Mel decided to surprise Morello, a delivery man, by stopping him outside the house, making him look away from his bike, putting a rubber duck in his basket and then making him drive into the grounds of the house, where she made him open the basket to discover the duck. This baffled everyone, especially Morello.

DID IT PAY OFF?: Yes. Despite being up against Noel's rubber duck wedding and Joe's rubber duck holiday in a yurt, somehow Mel bagged the five points, mostly because Greg enjoyed Morello's confusion.

RELEVANT QUOTE: 'Who the f*** is Morello?' – Greg Davies

4 / THE ALPINE DARLING

DISTANCE FROM HOUSE: 15 metres

EPISODE: Series 11, episode 4 ('Premature Conker')

CONTESTANT: Lee Mack

TASK: Get this sheet of loo roll as far away from here as possible

WHAT HAPPENED: Unable to break off the sheet of loo roll or remove the loo roll from the holder, Lee decided to take off the holder off the wall itself, before running out of the compound and asking a woman driving a car to take the loo roll as far away from the house as she could. The woman was not happy, but she did it, driving three miles away to Kew.

DID IT PAY OFF? Absolutely not. Lee's idea was solid, but in taking the holder off the wall, he had inexplicably taken the loo roll itself off the holder, instantly disqualifying himself. In Greg's words, he'd got himself on a police watchlist by scaring a woman in a car for nothing.

RELEVANT QUOTE: 'I could kill you, Alex.' – Lee Mack, seconds after disqualification

DISTANCE FROM HOUSE: 20 metres

EPISODE: Series 10, episode 5 ('I Hate Your Trainers')

CONTESTANT: Johnny Vegas

TASK: Bag the heaviest thing from the furthest distance

WHAT HAPPENED: Johnny decided to go get someone from outside the house to 'bag' (initially saying that he wanted to hit someone over the head and put them in there). He found a man who agreed (after Johnny assured him he'd be able to get to work for 12).

He placed the man mostly inside the bagging machine before attaching various items to him (a piece of plywood, a microwave, a pedal bin, a banjo). Eventually he pulled the man fully through the bagging machine, like a midwife bringing new life into the world.

DID IT PAY OFF?: No. The score was judged through weight and distance, and, while Johnny had bagged a large weight (a full-sized man), it was decreed he had only done it from 10cm, much to Johnny's understandable fury. As a result he got 1 point.

RELEVANT QUOTE: 'I'm officially sulking.' – Johnny Vegas, post-1 point

DISTANCE FROM HOUSE: 25 metres

EPISODE: Series 6, episode 2 ('Tarpeters')

CONTESTANT: Liza Tarbuck

TASK: Make this wind-up man go on an extraordinary journey

WHAT HAPPENED: Liza took an immediate disliking to the wind-up man, describing him as 'terse' before taking him outside the house and making him cross a very busy road on his penny farthing. The little man dodged a few cars before getting nicked by one. At this point, Liza decided it was better to put him out of his misery. As Alex watched on in horror, Liza stamped on the little man, smashing him to smithereens.

DID IT PAY OFF?: On the official *Taskmaster Podcast* afterwards, Liza revealed that she had wanted to get this task over with so that she could get a taxi home early. Not only did she get her wish, she also managed to get four points for her troubles.

RELEVANT QUOTE: 'I didn't like him.' – Liza Tarbuck, seconds after crushing the wind-up man to death

4 / THE ALPINE DARLING

DISTANCE FROM HOUSE: 30 metres

EPISODE: Series 16, episode 5 ('Languidly')

CONTESTANT: Sam Campbell

TASK: Choose a new nickname based on something you do in the next 20 minutes

WHAT HAPPENED: Sam asked if he could 'go out on the road,' which Alex said was allowed but not encouraged, and proceeded to ask random passers-by if they could coin a new nickname for him. After a few rejections, Sam found someone willing, who 'spontaneously' came up with the name 'Doctor Cigarettes' (suspiciously soon after Sam had whispered something in his ear).

DID IT PAY OFF? Yes. Sam scored 5 points ahead of Lucy '-fer the Rock God' Beaumont and Julian 'Butch' Clary, although no one was quite sure why, not even Greg.

RELEVANT QUOTE: 'Smoking kills ... weaklings!' – Sam Campbell (*Taskmaster* does not endorse smoking.)

DISTANCE FROM HOUSE: 161 metres (river bank)

EPISODE: Series 1, episode 4 ('Down an octave')

CONTESTANT: Tim Key

TASK: Make this block of ice completely disappear

WHAT HAPPENED: Tim put it in a wheelbarrow and carted it down to the river, where he threw it in. Alex stopped the clock once he could no longer see the ice cube, despite his reservations about whether or not he had actually made it disappear.

DID IT PAY OFF? No. Greg decided, quite rightly, that just because

Alex can't see something doesn't mean that it has disappeared and, despite an inventive attempt, Tim came last and got 1 point.

RELEVANT QUOTE: 'I don't think it's dumping because it's a bit like water, isn't it?' – Tim Key on the ethics of throwing an ice block into a river

DISTANCE FROM HOUSE: 161 metres (river bank)

EPISODE: Series 5, episode 1 ('Dignity Intact')

CONTESTANT: Mark Watson

TASK: Give Alex a special cuddle

WHAT HAPPENED: Mark checked on the Internet for what constituted a special cuddle and decided that location was key. He spent almost all of his 20-minute time limit walking Alex to the river, where he then showed him a picture of his wife, presented him with a Curly Wurly and some grapes, and gave him a hug where their legs got tangled up.

DID IT PAY OFF?: Mark did break new ground as the first contestant to leave the house in the first episode of a series, but ultimately Greg wasn't moved, scoring him joint last with Nish.

RELEVANT QUOTES: 'You googled "Two men cuddle by a river bank in darkness"?' – Aisling Bea. 'I've had to change my phone since, yes.' – Mark Watson

DISTANCE FROM HOUSE: 161 metres

EPISODE: Series 5, episode 8 ('Their Water's So Delicious')

CONTESTANT: Mark Watson

4 / THE ALPINE DARLING

TASK: Get a coconut as far away from the Taskmaster house as possible, without touching the ground

WHAT HAPPENED: Mark used a member of the production crew, Ariel, to give him a piggyback ride all the way to the riverbank. Once there, he chucked the coconut into the river, where it presumably floated out to sea.

DID IT PAY OFF?: No. Inexplicably, Mark made it to the river and then, forgetting that he wasn't allowed to touch the ground, asked Ariel to put him down before throwing the coconut. In another massive Watsonian waste of everyone's time, he received 0 points.

RELEVANT QUOTES: 'I don't want to exaggerate the importance of it psychologically, but it probably will be the last thing I think about before I die.' – Mark Watson, in the studio, on his blunder

DISTANCE FROM HOUSE: 161 metres (river bank)

EPISODE: Series 15, episode 5 ('Old Honkfoot')

CONTESTANT: Frankie Boyle

TASK: Fake something

WHAT HAPPENED: While Jenny faked a heart attack (2 points) and Kiell faked a hand (2 points), Frankie faked his death, leaving behind a note, blaming the British security forces and the creative team behind *Antiques Roadshow*. To complete the look, he left his clothes by the river bank and then sprinted, half-naked, up the bank.

DID IT PAY OFF?: Scaring a few joggers was worth the 5 points.

RELEVANT QUOTE: 'Like me, your body is so much more shocking than your suicide could ever be.' – Greg Davies

AN ABSOLUTE CASSEROLE

DISTANCE FROM HOUSE: 275 metres/3.9km/10.5km

EPISODE: Series 1, episode 5 ('Little Denim Shorts')

CONTESTANT: Roisin Conaty/Romesh Ranganathan/Frank Skinner

TASK: Get this boulder as far away from this place as possible

WHAT HAPPENED: Roisin spent half of her hour time limit trying to get a courier to deliver the boulder to Camber Sands. When this failed, she resorted to just pushing it down the road.

Like Roisin, Romesh had the idea of a courier. Unlike Roisin, he actually found one. He took his boulder on a wheelbarrow for 3.9km to find Mo, the courier, to drive it as far away from the house as possible.

Frank put his boulder in a wheelbarrow and wheeled it to Chiswick train station, where he then got on a train to Feltham, 6.5 miles away.

DID IT PAY OFF? For Roisin? No. Alex pointed out she moved it 300 yards, just short of her 200,000-yard target of Camber Sands – 1 point (which was the story of Roisin's time on the show).

For Romesh? No. Not only was Mo a bit late, meaning that Romesh spent 50 minutes of the task pushing the wheelbarrow and only 10 minutes driving the rock, but also he accidentally sent Mo in the wrong direction, back towards the house, cancelling out all his good work.

For Frank? Yes. Despite getting a bit of pushback from the train operating company about whether or not you can bring a fake boulder on a train, Frank managed to grab 4 points.

4 / THE ALPINE DARLING

RELEVANT QUOTES: 'Good morning, I'm trying to get a facsimile boulder onto a train.' – Frank Skinner, mid-task, to a person at the train station

'I wanted a day trip.' – Roisin Conaty's reason for choosing Camber Sands specifically

'Do you understand why I can't deal with Mo? Mo is a prick!' – Romesh Ranganathan, losing his patience with Mo

DISTANCE FROM HOUSE: 300 metres

EPISODE: Series 11, episode 2 ('The Lure of the Treacle Puppies')

CONTESTANT: Mike Wozniak

TASK: Make this balloon hover for 20 seconds

WHAT HAPPENED: Mike lost control of his balloon almost immediately. It soon flew over the fence and across the neighbouring golf course, getting trapped in some trees. Determined not to lose Alex's precious balloon, Mike jumped the fence (the first contestant ever to do so), sprinted across the golf course and retrieved the balloon, before completing the rest of the task (while sneering, as required).

DID IT PAY OFF?: Very much so. After Charlotte and Lee got disqualified for losing their balloons, he managed to come second. He scored 4 points, although Greg did point out that even in victory he 'looked like the head of department from a local council who'd just been fired.'

RELEVANT QUOTE: 'It could have been a mine shaft.' – Greg Davies, on what was on the other side of the fence

DISTANCE FROM HOUSE: 321 metres

EPISODE: Series 6, episode 4 ('BMXing!')

CONTESTANT: Tim Vine

TASK: Do something manly with this cardboard box

WHAT HAPPENED: Tim did what any red-blooded man would do – took the cardboard box to the side of the road, took off his shirt, stood in the box and did a series of muscle man poses as cars honked their horns happily.

DID IT PAY OFF?: He got 4 points, but so did three other contestants, meaning he actually came joint last.

RELEVANT QUOTE: 'At a time when men are under a lot of fire, what a wonderful display of manliness.' – Greg Davies

DISTANCE FROM HOUSE: 363 metres

EPISODE: Series 11, episode 4 ('Premature Conker')

CONTESTANT: Jamali Maddix

TASK: Get this sheet of loo roll as far away from here as possible

WHAT HAPPENED: Like Lee (see page 67), Jamali had the idea to take the loo roll holder off the wall. Unlike Lee, he didn't use tools (he just yanked it) and he didn't get disqualified. He put it in a bag, throwing it over the fence (several times, after tying it to a piece of string), before realising he could just hop the fence (the second contestant ever to do so) and walk with it to get more distance. He ended up putting it in a water fountain in the golf course, nearly 400 metres away.

DID IT PAY OFF?: With Lee's disqualification, Jamali got the 5 points.

4 / THE ALPINE DARLING

RELEVANT QUOTE: 'I got far and then I just kinda got bored so I came back.' – Jamali Maddix on his task-winning technique

DISTANCE FROM HOUSE: 3.2km

EPISODE: Series 4, episode 6 ('Spatchcock It')

CONTESTANT: Mel Giedroyc

TASK: Get this camel through the smallest gap

WHAT HAPPENED: Eschewing more conventional gaps, Mel made Alex drive them both to a nearby high street, where Mel got out the car and sprinted through the entrance of a Baby Gap (the smallest Gap of the Gap branded stores).

DID IT PAY OFF?: Yes. She received 5 points and she didn't have to destroy a blender (see Joe Lycett's attempt).

RELEVANT QUOTE: 'The security cameras will have recorded Mel Giedroyc running in with a camel and running out again.' – Alex Horne

DISTANCE FROM HOUSE: At least 3.4km

EPISODE: Series 3, episode 4 ('A Very Nuanced Character')

CONTESTANTS: Sara Pascoe, Dave Gorman, Al Murray, Rob Beckett

TASK: Spread your clothes as far and as wide as possible at your own expense

WHAT HAPPENED: Sara bolted out of the house, ran to the river, put her sock around a wooden block and threw it into the water, before sprinting to Kew Bridge rail station just before the time on the task ran out.

AN ABSOLUTE CASSEROLE

Dave tore his shirt in two and put one half of it in a metal tower in the house. He then ran out of the grounds of the house, got on a bus, left a sock and gave another sock to a man biking to East Sheen, before attempting to get another bus, which sadly didn't come before the time ran out.

Al hired two taxis to drive Alex and members of the production as far away from the house as they could get, where they then flung the clothes into the distance. Al then picked up his car from home, went for a little drive in the opposite direction and hung his jumper on a bollard.

Rob got Alex to drive him around suburban west London in his van, before taking off his clothes and throwing them out of the window, ending with his trousers.

DID IT PAY OFF?: Yes. All of them scored more than Paul Chowdhry, who chucked half his clothes over the fence and dotted the rest around the garden, meaning he spread them a total of 0.0001 square km.

RELEVANT QUOTE: 'None of this quite explains why you took a knife to one of your shirts.' – Greg Davies to Dave Gorman

'What price glory?' – Al Murray

'I'd always been warned of getting into a van with a man with a beard with no trousers on. But it was great.' – Rob Beckett

'I've just got what we were supposed to be doing!' – Sara Pascoe, in the studio, many many weeks after doing the task

4 / THE ALPINE DARLING

DISTANCE FROM HOUSE: 29km

EPISODE: Series 3, episode 1 ('A Pea in a Haystack')

CONTESTANT: Al Murray

TASK: Propel this pea the furthest and land it on the red carpet.

WHAT HAPPENED: Al threw his pea onto the red carpet before rolling up the carpet, bundling it into a taxi and telling the taxi driver to go up the M4 as far as they could. They eventually got to Slough.

DID IT PAY OFF? It cost £150, but he got the 5 points and discovered that he actually knew the taxi driver's niece (she's a GP in Croydon). The perfect afternoon.

RELEVANT QUOTE: 'Amazing watching someone pay £150 to take a pea to Slough.' – Alex Horne

TASKMASTER MAP OF THE UK
(As told by Taskmaster contestants)

1. **London:** Home of the Taskmaster house and the Taskmaster Hotel (opened 2023, closed 2023), birthplace of Katherine Parkinson, the first person to genetically engineer a spider out of a table

2. **West Sussex:** Birthplace of Little Alex Horne

3. **Chesham:** Home of the Mayor of Chesham and Chesham United; site of Hugh Dennis' wonder goal

4. **Gatwick Airport:** Home of the world-famous toilet that John Kearns threw a loo roll into from around 40 metres (not under competition rules)

5. **Wem:** Birthplace of the Taskmaster (no pilgrimages, please)

6. **Carmarthenshire:** Famed for terrible motivational ties, birthplace of notorious celebrity stalker and hider in closets, Rhod Gilbert

7. **Liverpool:** Birthplace of world-famous bearded patisserie expert, Liza Tarbuck

8. **Bolton:** Birthplace of the first person to attempt to hop over a river (unsuccessful), Sophie Willan

9. **South Shields:** Birthplace of the inventor of 'Sausage Mixer', Chris Ramsey

10. **Outside Glasgow:** Site of the famous battle between the Braveheart Duck and his sworn enemy, the Duck Catcher (Kiell Smith-Bynoe)

11. **Dumfries and Galloway:** Home of the biggest urinators in the British Isles (according to Bob Mortimer, 'because their water is so delicious … they literally cannae stop')

4 / THE ALPINE DARLING

12. **Whitby:** Final resting place of series 17 contestant Count Dracula
13. **Norfolk:** Site where Munya Chawawa saw the Norfolk Panther (debatable) and Smooth Rupert, the blackbird
14. **East Sussex:** Home of the smallest urinators in the British Isles (again, source, Bob Mortimer – good for harvesting a small amount of piss, e.g. for household use).

GIVE ME SOME STATS:
Is it better to be born by the sea?

Hypothesis

You have a better chance of winning *Taskmaster* if you were born by or live on the coast.

WHERE DOES THIS COME FROM?

A question from Ian, a listener to the *Taskmaster People's Podcast*, after he noticed that many champions come from seaside towns (such as former host Lou Sanders).

WHAT DO THE STATS SAY?

Strangely, the stats do actually bear this out. Contestants born fewer than 10 miles away from the coast have an average points-per-task score of 3.17, while contestants who are born more than 40 miles away from the coast are 0.2 points per task worse off, on 2.97.

The contestants who do the worst by this metric, though, are those born between 25 and 40 miles away from the coast. They are more than 0.3 points per task worse off, scoring 2.86.

Some of the highest scoring champions were born very close to the sea or large bodies of water. Series 14 high-scorers Dara Ó Briain and Sarah Millican were both born less than a mile away from the sea (in Bray and South Shields respectively), while Mae Martin was born in Toronto on Lake Ontario. The highest scorer of all time, John Robins, was born in Bristol, which is around 12 miles away from

4 / THE ALPINE DARLING

the coast, so you don't necessarily need to be right next to the sea to be a winner.

There are still champions within the landlocked group though. Kerry Godliman and Sam Campbell, winners in series 3 and series 16 respectively, were both born more than 40 miles away from the coast, while Morgana Robinson, winner in series 12, was born more than 104 miles away from the coast in the city of Shepparton in Victoria, Australia. However, they're still a good bit closer to the sea than the contestant who was born furthest away – Mawaan Rizwan, who was born in Lahore, Pakistan, which is over 750 miles away from the coast!

Why though? Why would being close to the sea make you good at *Taskmaster*? Who can say? Maybe a childhood near dangerous water makes contestants more resourceful and practical. Maybe it means they can more easily channel the spirit animal of *Taskmaster* (the duck). Maybe it's all just random and we're just looking for patterns in a meaningless set of data. Fingers crossed it's not the last one.

- Average points per task of contestants born more than 40 miles away from coast: 2.97 (24 contestants)
- Average points per task of contestants born between 25–40 miles away from coast: 2.86 (26 contestants)
- Average points per task of contestants born between 10–25 miles away from coast: 3.00 (20 contestants)
- Average points per task of contestants born less than 10 miles away from coast: 3.17 (15 contestants)

TRANSPORTATION IN TASKMASTER

There are times on *Taskmaster* when legs (no matter how tremendous) just won't do, and contestants need to get on their bikes and ride (to quote John Robins, probably). Here's a list of all the vehicles featured on the show. Which is the fastest? Hint: it's not Victoria Coren Mitchell on a bicycle.

Barge

EPISODE: Series 15, episode 1 ('The Curse of Politeness')

TOP SPEED: 4mph

KEY ATTRIBUTES: Extremely slow to turn; shouting 'Brace, brace' while driving into a wall does almost nothing to stop it

CONTESTANT BEST AT IT: Mae Martin

CONTESTANT WORST AT IT: Frankie Boyle

RELEVANT QUOTE: 'One on the bargepole, for me.' – Kiell Smith-Bynoe

Hoverboard

EPISODE: Series 11, episode 1 ('It's Not Your Fault')

TOP SPEED: 12mph

KEY ATTRIBUTES: Very, very unsteady and slow; does not respond to someone saying 'Tick-tock, race against the clock' at it

CONTESTANT BEST AT IT: Mike Wozniak

4 / THE ALPINE DARLING

CONTESTANT WORST AT IT: Mike Wozniak

RELEVANT QUOTE: 'It might be sensing my creeping sense of dread.' – Mike Wozniak

Street sweeper

EPISODE: Series 16, episode 9 ('Fagin at the Disco')

TOP SPEED: 14mph

KEY ATTRIBUTES: All drivers must pass a street-sweeping proficiency test; can cause road rage in Julian Clary

CONTESTANT BEST AT IT: Sue Perkins

CONTESTANT WORST AT IT: Julian Clary

RELEVANT QUOTE: 'You can't stop me! YOU CAN'T STOP ME!' – Susan Wokoma

Mobility scooter

EPISODE: Series 8, episode 10 ('Clumpy Swayey Clumsy Man')

TOP SPEED: 18mph

KEY ATTRIBUTES: Hard to find when blindfolded; can panic Alex when driven straight at a camera

CONTESTANT BEST AT IT: Iain Stirling

CONTESTANT WORST AT IT: Lou Sanders

RELEVANT QUOTE: 'If you put your hazards on you can do literally whatever you want.' – Joe Thomas

Steamroller

EPISODE: Series 9, episode 3 ('Five Miles Per Day')

TOP SPEED: 25mph

KEY ATTRIBUTES: Bad at directing anything towards a goal; good at crushing statues of unrequited love

CONTESTANT BEST AT IT: Rose Matafeo

CONTESTANT WORST AT IT: David Baddiel

RELEVANT QUOTE: 'He was travelling at five miles per day.' – Alex Horne, on David Baddiel's speed

Scooter

EPISODE: Series 11, episode 1 ('It's Not Your Fault')

TOP SPEED: 30mph

KEY ATTRIBUTES: Might make the user go 'wheeeee', especially if they are called Charlotte Ritchie; hard to ride while carrying plates in an apron

CONTESTANT BEST AT IT: Charlotte Ritchie

CONTESTANT WORST AT IT: Jamali Maddix

RELEVANT QUOTE: 'You could send me on one for miles and I would laugh the whole way.' – Charlotte Ritchie

Go kart

EPISODE: Series 13, episode 2 ('Birdy Hand Finger')

TOP SPEED: 35mph

KEY ATTRIBUTES: Hiding one behind a goal can outfox Chris Ramsey

4 / THE ALPINE DARLING

and Ardal O'Hanlon for longer than you'd think; at high speeds can turn Sophie Duker into a sheep

CONTESTANT BEST AT IT: Bridget Christie

CONTESTANT WORST AT IT: Judi Love

RELEVANT QUOTE: 'My tongue is a sort of throttle.' – Ardal O'Hanlon

Dinghy

EPISODE: Series 10, episode 2 ('A Documentary About a Despot')

TOP SPEED: 36.5 knots (42mph)

KEY ATTRIBUTES: Hard to steer, especially without water and in a warehouse; not particularly easy to store balls on

CONTESTANT BEST AT IT: Daisy May Cooper

CONTESTANT WORST AT IT: Mawaan Rizwan

RELEVANT QUOTE: 'This is dehumanising. Oh, you arsehole.' – Johnny Vegas

Bicycle

EPISODES: Series 11, episode 1; series 12, episode 4

TOP SPEED: 90mph

KEY ATTRIBUTES: Extremely hard to learn to ride in 15 minutes while being filmed for Channel 4

CONTESTANT BEST AT IT: Desiree Burch

CONTESTANT WORST AT IT: Morgana Robinson

RELEVANT QUOTES: 'Life is for living!' – Sarah Kendall, said out of fear that she was boring the crew senseless; 'I'm going to look like a bear in a circus.' – Desiree Burch, on riding a small bike

Alex's car

EPISODES: Series 4, episode 6; series 5, episode 6; series 6, episode 1; series 17, episode 1

TOP SPEED: 150mph

KEY ATTRIBUTES: Can pull Alice Levine's legs clean off; perfect for popping to a nearby BabyGap

PERSON BEST AT DRIVING IT: Alex Horne

PERSON WORST AT DRIVING IT: John Robins' egg

RELEVANT QUOTE: 'The strongest part of a car is famously the window.' – Greg Davies

TASKMASTER HALL OF GLORY
Most Times Last in a Task

NAME: Katherine Parkinson

NUMBER OF NON-TEAM TASKS SHE CAME LAST IN: 17

SERIES: 10

POINTS: 118 (2.31 points per task)

POSITION IN SERIES: Fifth, just 44 points behind the series winner

FUN FACT: Katherine is one of a few contestants to never win a prize task in her series, along with Alice Levine (series 6), Joe Thomas (series 8), Munya Chawawa (series 14), Ivo Graham (series 15) and Morgana Robinson (series 12 champion).

GREATEST ACHIEVEMENT: Creating a genuinely excellent marble run that used Newton's laws of motion to go from one end of the room to the other, possibly by accident.

LOWEST MOMENTS: Greg being mean about her masks; not knowing how to make a catapult to fire a shoe into a bath.

RELEVANT QUOTE: 'It's a shame that my hands aren't my feet.'

TASKMASTER MAP OF THE WORLD

Number of countries in the world according to Mark Watson – 92; number of countries in the world according to Bob Mortimer – 3.

1. **England:** Birthplace of 63 contestants and Little Alex Horne
2. **Scotland:** Birthplace of three contestants (Iain Stirling, Frankie Boyle, Fern Brady)
3. **Wales:** Birthplace of three contestants (Rhod Gilbert, Sian Gibson, Katy Wix) and the Taskmaster; ancestral home of Owain ap Gruffydd, to whom Greg Davies may or may not be related
4. **Ireland:** Birthplace of four contestants (Aisling Bea, Ardal O'Hanlon, Dara Ó Briain, Joanne McNally); home of the greatest bobsleigh team in the world (according to Aisling Bea); in Ireland, they shake hands really weirdly (according to Joanne McNally)
5. **France:** Birthplace of French cinema, as pioneered by Sally Phillips in 'Le Chat Est Boing Boing'; in France, they pronounce Hugh Dennis, 'Hugh Dennis'
6. **Japan:** Birthplace of the yardstick of failure (Ivo Graham); flag made from a dyed red pancake covered in ketchup (designed by Rob Beckett)
7. **Pakistan:** Birthplace of the great helium egg scientist, Mawaan Rizwan
8. **Malaysia:** Birthplace of barge menace Jenny Eclair

4 / THE ALPINE DARLING

9. **United States:** Birthplace of lasso expert David Baddiel, and Desiree Burch; home of Mount Rushmore, the little-known landmark that inspired Katy Wix's mashed potato Mount Rushmore

10. **Australia:** Birthplace of three *Taskmaster* champions (Sarah Kendall, Morgana Robinson, Sam Campbell); birthplace of hated enemy of Julian Clary, Pluck-a-duck

11. **Canada:** Birthplace of two Taskmaster champions, Katherine Ryan and Mae Martin

12. **New Zealand:** Birthplace of *Junior Taskmaster* and notorious shed mis-pronouncer, Rose Matafeo; country that Kiell Smith-Bynoe's very small imaginary friend Louis always wanted to visit (before he was killed falling down a plughole drain)

13. **Hong Kong:** Birthplace of Alex Horne's mother, Sally Phillips

14. **Indonesia:** Origin of a toy chariot that Phil Wang bought for 100,000 rupees (haggled down from 100,000 rupees).

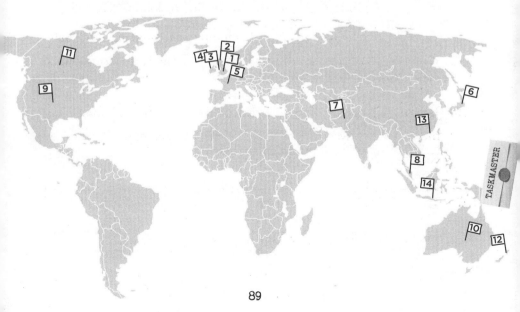

INTERNATIONAL CONTESTANTS

In all there have been 16 contestants born outside the UK on *Taskmaster*. Despite their lack of home advantage, they are actually *more* successful than their British counterparts: they have a higher average points per task score, and have produced six champions (and one champion of champions). Here's a rundown of some of the most successful international superstars.

Mae Martin

COUNTRY OF BIRTH: Canada

SERIES: 15

POINTS PER TASK: 3.48 (third overall)

NATIONAL PRIDE: Highest margin of victory in *Taskmaster* history (16 points); can communicate with the dead (fraudulently)

LOST IN TRANSLATION: Claimed 'humiliate' is spelt 'humliate' in Canada to win a task (didn't get away with it)

IRRELEVANT QUOTE: 'I beaver away … famously.' (series 15, episode 2)

Joanne McNally

COUNTRY OF BIRTH: Republic of Ireland

SERIES: 17

POINTS PER TASK: 3.42 (sixth overall)

NATIONAL PRIDE: Nearly went the entire season without getting disqualified; 'Custard Mustard Oh My' World Champion

4 / THE ALPINE DARLING

- **LOST IN TRANSLATION:** Her Che Guevara balloon prize task for 'most extraordinary picture' baffled and confused everyone, herself included
- **IRRELEVANT QUOTE:** 'What's your salary? Don't lie. Don't lie to your mother.' (series 17, episode 3)

Morgana Robinson

COUNTRY OF BIRTH: Australia

SERIES: 12

POINTS PER TASK: 3.36 (eighth overall)

NATIONAL PRIDE: Series 12 winner; knows Vic Reeves well enough to get some of his hair for the show

LOST IN TRANSLATION: Greg was not on board with her prize task of 40 chips on a towel, despite her inventing a great chip tagline ('Chips are dope!')

IRRELEVANT QUOTE: 'Where is the little f***er?' (series 12, episode 1)

Katherine Ryan

COUNTRY OF BIRTH: Canada

SERIES: 2

POINTS PER TASK: 3.36 (ninth overall)

NATIONAL PRIDE: First female winner of *Taskmaster*; can rap about anything, including the Mayor of Chesham's testicles; willing to ruin her family's life for *Taskmaster*

LOST IN TRANSLATION: Simply will not participate in the traditional English pastime of eating a raw egg

IRRELEVANT QUOTE: 'I just don't care where the ball goes.' – on why she doesn't like sport (series 2, episode 1)

Sam Campbell
COUNTRY OF BIRTH: Australia
SERIES: 16
POINTS PER TASK: 3.22 (fourteenth overall)
NATIONAL PRIDE: Second youngest champion in show's history; only contestant willing to bribe a ten-year-old to win
LOST IN TRANSLATION: Can be easily tricked into doing someone else's task for them (especially by Susan Wokoma)
IRRELEVANT QUOTE: 'Are you a child of divorce?' (series 16, episode 1)

FRED THE SWEDE
By Alex

One of my (many) favourite tasks came in series 1, episode 5. The wording was as follows:

    Make this Swedish person blush as deeply as possible.
    You have ten minutes.
    Your time starts now.

The task attempt eventually yielded the episode title after Tim Key entreated our Swedish person to think about his 'little denim shorts', but how did we find our blusher in the first place? As so often with *Taskmaster*, there was no planning, no official meeting and a lot of happenstance.

The one thing we all knew was that we needed someone for whom a blush would be visible on camera. Leaning into our knowledge of national stereotypes, this led us to think that a Scandinavian person might be useful. 'Does anyone know a Scandinavian person?' We asked each other. 'Oh, I do!' I said. Because I knew Fred.

Alongside assisting the Taskmaster, I am the nominal frontman of the band (and theme tune masters) the Horne Section. We've been performing together for as long as *Taskmaster* has existed with largely the same line-up, but very occasionally a band member has to miss a gig because of other commitments. In this circumstance a 'dep' steps in, and we all realise how disposable we are.

Ben (our drummer) has seldom been required elsewhere, but it has happened and when it does we often get a handsome Swede to fill his boots and hold his sticks. Please welcome Fred to the stage!

Ben and Fred had known each other for years, as all jazz musicians do, and lived in the same corner of London. Fred slotted nicely into our bizarre band dynamic and I was always more happy than I should have been when I received a message from Ben saying he was having trouble with the date of a gig.

So, when asked if I knew a Scandinavian person, I remembered Fred. He's a classic Swede – blond, pale, steely, mostly unruffled – but I was sure I remembered him going red on stage at some point in the past.

I called Fred. I explained myself as briefly as possible. He said, 'Sure.' I hung up.

I followed up with an email:

'I hope it all made sense on the phone. Basically, you'll be in a room. A comedian will come in and they have ten minutes to try to make you blush. That's it! I have no idea what they'll do, but they'll be on camera and they'll be trying to be funny.'

Fred said, 'Sure.'

We had our man. He turned up on five separate occasions, sat in the lab and waited for our unsuspecting comedians. Neither he nor they knew what was going to happen, but after an unprecedented couple of weeks Fred had been nuzzled by Romesh, shared fantasies with Josh and licked by Frank. Tim talked to him about those tiny shorts and the winner of the task, Roisin, made him put his head between his legs while asking where her third breast would be if she were to have an extra one. 'Sangria red' was what he went, according to Greg, and Fred became something of a hero.

It wasn't just the team who wanted him back in future series. We got many messages asking about our delightful Swede and despite now living back in his homeland, Fred tells me he is still regularly stopped

4 / THE ALPINE DARLING

and politely asked about his time on the show. He finds it a little embarrassing, he says. 'Do you blush?' I ask. 'Of course', says Fred.

Fred went on to appear in four other series of the show, most recently series 13, where the likes of Ardal O'Hanlan and Judi Love attempted to learn his language and have a chat with him. That's another of my (many) favourite tasks and I don't think it would surprise anyone if Fred returns to do more things he never expected to do for the entertainment of the world.

FACTFILE FOR FRED THE SWEDE

Name: Fred the Swede
Nationality: Swedish
Really: Yes (as verified by Noel Fielding)
Date of birth: 27 August, 1981
Profession: Painter-decorator/musician
Marital status: Single (as of 2017)
Number of task appearances: Five (and a tiebreak, as a picture):
- Make this Swedish person blush (series 1, episode 5)
- Find out information from this Swedish person who cannot communicate in English (series 2, episode 1)
- Balance your swedes on the Swede (series 3, episode 1)
- While maintaining eye contact and small talk with this Swede put on a wetsuit. (series 4, episode 5)
- Learn Swedish (series 13, episode 8)

Has he watched 1970s soft porn films? No

Has he ever been handcuffed, whipped, smothered in chocolate, licked, kicked or kissed? No

Knowledge of Claudia Winkleman: Non-existent.

Would he like to see someone with three breasts? Yes

Would he like to see someone with four breasts? No

Father's profession: Decorator

Greatest fear: Failure

How would he describe Doc Brown? 'You've got short hair.'

How would he describe Jon Richardson? 'Kind eyes, small beard, I would say you're shorter than average.'

Effect on Jon Richardson's self-esteem: Not good

Favourite food: Hamburgers, boiled potatoes, cream sauce, fried onions and lingonberries

Favourite type of quiche: Unspecified (much to Joe Lycett's frustration)

Does he like Swedish food? No, he thinks it's quite boring

Is he into McDonalds? No

Number of swedes Al Murray can balance on him: 15 (world record)

Favourite colour to paint in: Blue

Last thing he painted blue: A kitchen

Does he want to stay in touch with Noel Fielding? Yes

Does he know he actually won't stay in touch with Noel Fielding? Yes

Does he like football? Yes

Does Chris Ramsey like to talk about football with him? No

Reaction to a random comedian telling him she is pregnant: Polite confusion

Reaction to Irish comedians singing folk songs about being drunk and letting the sick fall down like hail: Polite confusion

Shades of red he goes when he blushes:

    Jasmine shimmer (Josh Widdicombe, 1 point)

    Cherry blossom (Tim Key, 2 points)

    Fantasy rose (Frank Skinner, 3 points)

    Puce (Romesh Ranganathan, 4 points)

    Ballet slipper/sangria (Roisin Conaty, 5 points)

Edinburgh Task 3: How Did It Go?

German Comedy Ambassador Henning Wehn won this task with his vague:

'HE DID IT AGAIN'

Which turned out to be stunningly accurate as Phil 'The Power' Taylor successfully defended his Darts World Championship title at London's Alexandra Palace on 3 January.

Second place was Stuart Goldsmith's more ambitious offering:

'MOON-CHEESE! – the French invade the moon/ Branson makes mad cheddar out of moon enterprises'

There weren't any headlines in any newspapers that bore any resemblance to this, but I appreciated the creativity. Also, by this stage it's fair to say that nearly all the contestants were lagging behind in terms of task deadlines, something that is fairly representative of elements like the prize task in the production of the television show today.

EDINBURGH TASK 4
4 December 2009

Well then.

Now that you all know where we stand (way behind Mr H. Wehn), it's time for your fourth task:

MASSIVE CHRISTMAS PRESENTS

Send me something LARGE through the post.

The five LARGEST things will win the points (10 for the biggest, then 8, 6, 4, 2).

You must send your LARGE thing to 1 The Street, Town, County PO1 2CO.

*IMPORTANT: IT MUST ARRIVE BY 20 DECEMBER.
YOU DON'T HAVE LONG.

Also, please send me your own weight, in stones, pounds or kilograms.

Sorry for this intrusion. I won't publish the figure anywhere I promise. But it is important. Thank you.

And good luck.

The Taskmaster

5

AN ORDERLY SPECIES

TASKMASTER AND SOCIETY

What is a society? Is it the global community all working together for the betterment of the human race, guided by the true visionaries (think Emmeline Pankhurst, Rosa Parks, Malala Yousafzai, Greg Davies)? Or are we all just individuals scrabbling at each other's eyes in a desperate attempt to rise to the top/earn more points than Richard Herring? This section won't answer that question, but it does feature a dancing elephant, which is almost the same thing.

WORKING TOGETHER: TOP TEAMS

Some teams are kindred spirits, like David Baddiel and Jo Brand or Hugh Dennis and Mel Giedroyc. Some provide the father you never knew you needed, like Frankie Boyle to Ivo Graham or Richard Osman to Jon Richardson. And some are formed because the producers want to make Dara Ó Briain's head explode by putting him with John Kearns and Fern Brady. Here's a list of the best teams.

Series 16: Sam Campbell, Julian Clary, Lucy Beaumont

TEAM TASK POINTS: 23

TOTAL TEAM TASKS: 6

POINTS PER TEAM TASK: 3.83

BEST MOMENT: Thinking their way through the first team task and making the most 'connections' between themselves by cutting off locks of their hair and holding it in a clip. As Sam said, they're like the divers that saved the boys in the cave – clinical guys, but capable of just amazing things.

WORST MOMENT: Running the Taskmaster Hotel into the ground, with Lucy playing the French horn, Sam breaking into the customers' rooms to watch them get changed and Julian impassively allowing the whole house to burn down ('Oh is there a fire? How awful.')

RELEVANT QUOTE: 'Lovely legs, Sir!' – Lucy Beaumont to the customer at the Taskmaster Hotel, about five times

5 / AN ORDERLY SPECIES

Series 14: Sarah Millican, Munya Chawawa

TEAM TASK POINTS: 36

TOTAL TEAM TASKS: 9

POINTS PER TEAM TASK: 4.00

BEST MOMENT: Winning the 'Come up with a secret language that doesn't use words' task by assigning assorted bells words like 'lick', 'punch', 'gently', 'hard', 'medium'.

WORST MOMENT: The task where they had to transfer a feather into a bath without talking. The leafblower was, despite Sarah's excitement at finding it, entirely useless and they ended up taking an astonishing 24 minutes 25 seconds, when the other team had done it in less than 8 minutes.

RELEVANT QUOTE: 'It's like having a bairn, I imagine, where you're just like, look at his little face!' – Sarah Millican on her relationship with Munya

Series 13: Sophie Duker, Bridget Christie, Judi Love

TEAM TASK POINTS: 26

TOTAL TEAM TASKS: 6

POINTS PER TEAM TASK: 4.33

BEST MOMENT: As 'The House Queens' in the final task of the series: Judi Love's beautiful vocals on the hook, Sophie Duker's unstoppable percussive beats and lyrics ('Gonna cook you some pasta', and the whistling madness of Bridget Christie.

WORST MOMENT: The go-kart and making Sophie scream like a scared lamb as she tried to score a goal.

RELEVANT QUOTE: 'Eat your f***ing worms!' – Bridget Christie at the worst stag-do ever

Series 17: John Robins, Joanne McNally, Sophie Willan

TEAM TASK POINTS: 33
TOTAL TEAM TASKS: 7
POINTS PER TEAM TASK: 4.71

BEST MOMENT: When the teams had to make the most number of moves on the movement circles (in a task that was effectively darts mixed with Twister). John had the darts down (captain of the college team), throwing with unerring accuracy to pick out moves for the very flexible Joanne to carry out, while Sophie ... chucked a water bottle a bit. They ended up making 43 different movements – more than eight times as many as the team of two, the biggest margin of victory in a team task ever.

WORST MOMENT: The team task in episode 1 where they had only just met, but were separated by a fence, could only communicate in two-word bursts and had to draw an animal doing a surprising thing. Car crash.

RELEVANT QUOTE: 'UMBRELLA' – Sophie Willan, subtly completing her secret task to say umbrella

Series 15: Mae Martin, Kiell Smith-Bynoe, Jenny Eclair

TEAM TASK POINTS: 42

TOTAL TEAM TASKS: 8

POINTS PER TEAM TASK: 5.25

BEST MOMENT: The live task from episode 5, when they had to stuff stuff inside Kiell's waders and then work out how many items they stuffed. Get it right, they doubled their points tally. Get it wrong and the points would go to the other team. In a moment of high drama, Mae guessed 29 ... and got it absolutely right.

WORST MOMENT: Jenny and Mae's high-pitched voices telling an increasingly frustrated Kiell how to pick up spoons.

RELEVANT QUOTE: 'AQUA-MARINE' – Jenny Eclair during the 'Write the most soporific lullaby task,' yelling colours at a baby

TASKMASTER HALL OF GLORY
Highest Scores in an Episode

NAME: Katherine Ryan

HIGHEST SCORE IN AN EPISODE: 30 (5.00 points per task) (series 2, episode 3)

SERIES POINTS: 94 (3.36 points per task)

POSITION IN SERIES: First, 4 points ahead of Jon Richardson

CONTROVERSIAL FACT: Going into the final task of this episode, Katherine was on 15 points – a fairly unimpressive 3.00 points per task. But in the final task – where contestants had to throw rabbits into a hat – she scored 15 points, much to the fury of Jon Richardson and Richard Osman.

NAME: Dara Ó Briain

HIGHEST SCORE IN AN EPISODE: 30 (6.00 points per task) (series 10, episode 2)

SERIES POINTS: 184 (3.68 points per task)

POSITION IN SERIES: First

FUN FACT: Dara became the first ever contestant on *Taskmaster UK* to get a perfect episode – he won every task here, including the live team task (where he was paired with John Kearns and Fern Brady, and had to explain how helicopters worked in two words).

RELEVANT QUOTE: 'Ascend vertically!'

GOING IT ALONE:
A BRIEF HISTORY OF INDIVIDUAL TASKS

Sometimes, due to 'admin errors', Alex sets a task for one person and forgets to set it for the others. What's more, they're usually the most time-consuming and annoying tasks – what are the chances?

Josh Widdicombe

TASK: Count the beans in this tin of baked beans; count the hoops in this tin of spaghetti hoops; count the grains of rice in this bag of rice

EPISODE: Series 1, episode 4 ('Down an Octave')

WHAT HAPPENED: The Taskmaster is a fastidious guy, so wanted to check just how many beans there were in a tin. Up steps Josh Widdicombe, who dutifully sat in the lab one day to count them all out – not knowing he was the only one in his series to be tasked with it. Josh was understandably furious, especially when the show revealed that they had also tasked him with counting out hoops in a spaghetti hoop tin and (most upsetting of all) grains of rice in a rice packet.

POINTS: 1 – which seems harsh, but became relevant when Josh won the series by a single point in the final episode

RELEVANT QUOTES: 'How in the first episode where I'm actually winning, do I feel the saddest I've ever felt?' – Josh Widdicombe

Jon Richardson

TASK: Prove how strong you are; enjoy this clip of the *Taskmaster*; perform a recognisable rendition of the *William Tell Overture* using just your hands and cheeks; present a makeup tutorial

EPISODE: Series 2, episode 4 ('Welcome to Rico Face')

WHAT HAPPENED: The other four contestants on the series were set the task 'Set a fun task' that could be no longer than a minute, not knowing that Jon Richardson would be subjected to all of them in a four-minute barrage. The makeup tutorial was perhaps the most difficult. Jon came out with great insights like 'This is for making your cheeks nice and pink, if your cheeks aren't pink enough,' and at one point said that the lipstick 'tasted horrible'.

POINTS: 4 – he had a terrible time, but guessed which contestant set which task perfectly

RELEVANT QUOTE: 'And that concludes this month's make-up tutorial: how to degrade yourself in just under a minute.' – Jon Richardson

Paul Chowdhry

TASK: Have the most fun on a bouncy castle for one hour

EPISODE: Series 3, episode 4

WHAT HAPPENED: Paul, the most misanthropic man to ever be on *Taskmaster*, was given a bouncy castle and made to have fun. Unsurprisingly, it did not work. He looked like a divorced dad at a soft play.

POINTS: 0

RELEVANT QUOTE: 'Are you kidding? I f***ing love him.' – Greg Davies on whether he was happy with Paul's attempt

5 / AN ORDERLY SPECIES

Mel Giedroyc

TASK: Hide this ball from Alex

EPISODE: Series 4, episode 6 ('Spatchcock It')

WHAT HAPPENED: In an attempt to push Mel, the nicest woman in the world, to her limits, Greg set her an impossible task: to hide a massive inflatable ball from Alex without damaging it. The usually calm Mel was instantly panicked, trying to push the ball over a fence (while yelling bollocks over and over), before Alex came out and found the ball immediately. It was made more annoying by the fact that they had also set Mel another task to inflate the ball in the house, before making her score a goal with it in the garden (meaning she had to deflate it again to get it through the door).

POINTS: 0 – but Mel was still happy

RELEVANT QUOTES: 'She also used the word "heck".' – Alex Horne
'And of course that's Mel's equivalent of BLEEP.' – Greg Davies

Sally Phillips

TASK: Make the most fish puns. Most fish puns wins

EPISODE: Series 5, episode 8 ('Their Water's So Delicious')

WHAT HAPPENED: Sally had a minute to make as many fish puns as she could and she made a great fist at it (including the excellent 'I've got my herring a bun' and the less excellent 'I cod do this'). It then transpired she'd been up against Alex the whole time, who had spent the entire series throwing in fish puns whenever he was with Sally ('I've already got a haddock', 'Here's a tuna baked beans', 'there are three tasks in a roe for you'). The 'winner' of that task, he gleefully put his own face on the scoreboard (which Greg then forced him to take off immediately).

POINTS: 0

RELEVANT QUOTE: 'I just thought you were bad at speaking.' – Sally Phillips on why she hadn't noticed all of Alex's fish puns

Mike Wozniak

TASK: Fart

EPISODE: Series 11, episode 6

WHAT HAPPENED: Mike was tasked with farting on an airplane. It was supposed to be a simple task, but Mike's digestive system was not playing ball. After a few hours of trying, the crew had to go to lunch and the task was seemingly abandoned. However, at the conclusion of another task, Mike announced that something had changed and that he was ready to give it another go. After a real effort, there was a disgusting tiny little pop and Mike had completed the task. Greg assumed that Mike had shat himself, but Mike revealed a much darker truth – he had inadvertently dislodged a haemorrhoid that had been in there for some time. I am so sorry that I had to type those words.

POINTS: 1 – but he simultaneously deserved more and less

RELEVANT QUOTE: 'It's an absolute casserole down there.' – Mike Wozniak

5 / AN ORDERLY SPECIES

Sam Campbell

'TASK': Stand up and shout 'mice' whenever you see or hear mice; sit down and whisper 'fish' whenever you see or hear a fish

ACTUAL TASK: Make mischief

EPISODE: Series 16, episode 2

ACTUAL CONTESTANT: Susan Wokoma

WHAT HAPPENED: Sam was sent into the toilet to complete a 20-minute 'task': to shout mice when he saw mice and whisper fish when he saw a fish. Sam took to the task well, witnessing 133 mice and 97 fish across 20 minutes, and even started drawing his own fish and mice on Alex's clipboard. Only afterwards did he discover that it wasn't actually a real task, but one that Susan Wokoma had mischievously invented for the 'Make mischief' task – and the animals were selected because 'mice' and 'fish' was an anagram of mischief. Glorious.

POINTS: 0 for Sam, 5 for Susan

RELEVANT QUOTE: 'How deep does this go, Wokoma?!' – Sam Campbell

FACTS ABOUT EGGS 1

🥚 Did you know that the word 'egg' features in 73 out of 160 episodes of *Taskmaster*? If you're watching an episode of *Taskmaster*, there is a 46 per cent chance that the show you're watching will feature an egg.

🥚 By comparison, the word 'chicken' features in just 42 episodes, meaning there's a 26 per cent chance that any random episode you're watching will feature a chicken.

🥚 Only one episode in the entire history of the show features the word 'girdle', so if you love eggs, are neither bothered nor unbothered about chickens, but hate girdles, then you'll probably be in luck watching a random episode. Unless you watch series 17, episode 5. Lots of girdle chat in that.

🥚 British people use thirteen billion eggs every year, sometimes going up to fourteen billion if Romesh Ranganathan is doing an egg-based task.

HOW TO GREET ALEX

Greeting people can be difficult. Sometimes you can fail to realise that the person who has entered the grounds is a person you're supposed to greet and not just some bloke delivering something (see Frankie Boyle meeting Ivo Graham for the team tasks in series 15). Sometimes your very presence can terrify a person to their very core (see Richard Herring meeting Daisy May Cooper for the team tasks in series 10). Fortunately, greeting Alex is a much simpler affair. Our handy guide to greeting him will see you right! Or it'll get you barred from the Little Alex Horne Assistants' Day celebrations, who can say.

The Alice Levine

METHOD: Call Alex a different adorable nickname every time you see him

EXAMPLES: 'Alright fittie?', 'Hi blossom!', 'Hey girl!' (to a bearded man in his late thirties), 'Hi babycakes!', 'Hi cherub!' 'Hello my little ferret!', 'Hi possums!', 'BELLA!'

ALEX HORNE REACTION: Confusion mixed with happiness at being given some rare affection

RECOMMENDED: Yes, although it makes it much harder to swear at him when you have to pop a bubble with your nose.

The James Acaster

METHOD: Ignore any niceties from Alex at all times

TECHNIQUE: Wordlessly flick open the task while avoiding any kind of acknowledgement with cold, dead eyes (which are circles)

ALEX HORNE REACTION: Hopeful that maybe today would be the day James said hello to him, followed by crushing disappointment

RECOMMENDED: No, as it probably makes Alex enjoy the tasks where you have to tie yourself up and hop helplessly through the house all the more.

The Joe Lycett

METHOD: Shake hands with Alex while tickling their palm and maintaining eye contact for a full three minutes

TECHNIQUE: Start gently, and then speed up, faster and faster

ADVANCED LEVEL: Whenever the greetee starts to speak, go, 'Shh,' and then, quietly, 'I love you.' They are required to say it back to you

ALEX HORNE REACTION: Palpable discomfort. In Greg's words, 'He hated every second of that.'

RECOMMENDED: Yes, if you never want Alex to look you in the eyes again.

The Lolly Adefope

METHOD: Go up to Alex and give him £20, a breath mint and codeine

TECHNIQUE: Be extremely blatant about your tactic of bribing your colleague with money and drugs. Any attempt to hide the corruption will ultimately look worse

5 / AN ORDERLY SPECIES

ALEX HORNE REACTION: Delighted – he had bad breath, a headache and Greg doesn't pay him

WHAT ALEX DID WITH THE MONEY: Gave it to Greg

WHAT GREG DID WITH THE MONEY: Bought some ham

RECOMMENDED: Yes, but it won't stop Greg marking you down for being so darn young.

The Sally Phillips

METHOD: Call Alex the wrong name (Alan)

TECHNIQUE: Just do it very casually and hope he won't call you up on it (he will)

ALEX HORNE REACTION: Genuinely quite annoyed

RECOMMENDED: Irrelevant, because you can pretty much get away with anything (even having it off with a water cooler in a caravan).

The Nick Mohammed

METHOD: Call Alex the wrong name (Greg)

TECHNIQUE: Do it midway through a task and then feel terrible about it to the point that you stop doing the task

ALEX HORNE REACTION: Genuinely quite proud that anyone could ever, ever confuse him with Greg Davies

RECOMMENDED: Not if you want to stay on Greg's good side.

STAYING AT HOME
All the hometasking tasks

During the first Covid lockdown, in March 2020, I was quite surprised when I received a few messages from society.

By society what I mean is that a handful of parents got in contact to ask if I could help them in this unprecedented global meltdown. Because, as well as witnessing the horrifying worldwide health situation, these people had recently, suddenly, become teachers to their own children. Their homes were now schools. They were almost immediately at their wits' end.

I phoned the Taskmaster team and asked permission to dish out a task. They granted the request and the Taskmaster Himself agreed to judge the results. But, like the show itself, what started as a one-off quickly snowballed into something that kept many people's spirits up, not least the Taskmaster hosts.

These are the tasks that were tackled by thousands of people both in the UK and across the globe. Please do go to the Taskmaster YouTube channel to see some quite extraordinary task attempts.

TASK #1 – 23 MARCH 2020
Throw a piece of A4 paper into a bin. Most spectacular throw wins.

TASK #2 – 25 MARCH 2020
Turn your bathroom into the sort of venue you might visit for a great night out. Best bathroom conversion wins.

5 / AN ORDERLY SPECIES

TASK #3 - 27 MARCH 2020

Make the best dancing elephant.

TASK #4 - 30 MARCH 2020

Camouflage yourself and then reveal yourself. Best camouflage wins.

TASK #5 - 1 APRIL 2020

Turn your kitchen into a sporting arena and create the most epic moment of sporting glory.

TASK #6 - 6 APRIL 2020

Do something extraordinary with a pair of trousers. Most extraordinary thing done with a pair of trousers wins.

TASK #7 - 8 APRIL 2020

Silently recreate an iconic movie moment. You may not use stop motion or computer animation. Most ambitious and enjoyable silent recognisable movie moment re-enactment wins.

TASK #8 - 13 APRIL 2020

Turn your bed into something that isn't a bed. Best bed development wins.

TASK #9 - 15 APRIL 2020

Become a superhero and demonstrate your superpowers. Best superhero wins.

TASK #10 – 20 APRIL 2020

Put something surprising under a sheet. Then reveal the surprising thing from under the sheet. Most surprising thing revealed from under a sheet wins!

TASK #11 – 22 APRIL 2020

Make and demonstrate the best method of transport inside your home. You must be able to get in or on your method of transport.

TASK #12 – 27 APRIL 2020

Re-enact a momentous moment from history. Most authentic and powerful historical re-enactment wins.

TASK #13 – 29 APRIL 2020

Make a really, really big version of something that is usually quite small, then demonstrate your really, really big version in action. Most ridiculously oversized working item wins.

TASK #14 – 4 MAY 2020

Put on an item of clothing in the most unusual way. Most unusual donning of clothing wins.

TASK #15 – 6 MAY 2020

Demonstrate the most extreme housework. Most extreme housework wins.

TASK #16 – 13 MAY 2020

Make and show off your best invention. Best invention wins.

5 / AN ORDERLY SPECIES

TASK #17 – 20 MAY 2020

Make yourself look exactly like a famous person doing an unlikely activity. The first name of the famous person and the activity must begin with the same letter (e.g. Greg Davies: glass-blowing). Best combination of celebrity look-a-like and unlikely activity wins.

TASK #18 – 27 MAY 2020

Look incredibly cool in a slow-motion video. Most incredibly cool person in a slow-motion video wins.

TASK #19 – 3 JUNE 2020

Do the most amazing thing with one hand on your hip at all times. Most amazing thing done with one hand on your hip at all times wins.

TASK #20 – 10 JUNE 2020

Make a big and expressive face out of things from your house. Biggest and most expressive face wins.

TASK #21 – 14 JANUARY 2021

Design and demonstrate the best quick-change outfit. Best and quickest quick change outfit wins.

TASK #22 – 21 JANUARY 2021

Make the best domino rally. Best domino rally wins.

TASK #23 – 28 JANUARY 2021

Make the most striking water feature. Most striking water feature wins.

TASK #24 – 4 FEBRUARY 2021
Throw something into something. Most unbelievable throw wins.

TASK #25 – 11 FEBRUARY 2021
Do the most powerful thing with your little finger. Most powerful thing done with your little finger wins.

TASK #26 – 18 FEBRUARY 2021
Stage a realistic blooper from a home movie.

TASK #27 – 25 FEBRUARY 2021
Physically recreate a classic computer game. Best recreation wins.

TASK #28 – 4 MARCH 2021
Tell the Taskmaster you love him in the most meaningful way.

TASK #29 – 1 MAY 2021
Construct the best fort and spend the night in it. You must not use your bed in the construction of your fort. Best fort wins.

TASK #30 – 25 OCTOBER 2021
Make and demonstrate the spookiest animal using stuff from your kitchen.

TASKS THAT TOOK LONGER THAN ANYONE THOUGHT POSSIBLE

Some tasks go on for so long that they can break a contestant's brain. You can see a moment in their eyes where they suddenly become painfully aware of what they're doing and how they're wasting their precious time on earth to satisfy the whim of a dictator from Wem. Their minds suddenly fill with questions like 'What is life?' 'What is existence?' 'Is there a duck on my face?' 'No, seriously, is there a duck on my face?' (Those last two might just be Judi Love.) Here are some of the moments when contestants stared into the abyss of time itself and came out forever changed. Or their eyes just hurt a bit.

Longest and best task attempt, no. 1

TASK: Don't blink

EPISODE: Series 7, episode 7 ('The Perfect Stuff')

CONTESTANT: Rhod Gilbert

TIME: 7 minutes, 10 seconds

METHODOLOGY: Rhod pulled his eyes open with his hands, before attempting to use gaffer tape to keep his eyelids up. At one point he tipped the tears out by jerking his head to the ground. It was disgusting.

SCORE: 5

RELEVANT QUOTE: 'Like something from *A Clockwork Orange*. Honestly, hand on heart, fifteen years of friendship, that's the most impressed I've ever been with you.' – Greg Davies

Longest and best task attempt, no. 2

TASK: Hide from Alex in a game of hide and seek

EPISODE: Series 4, episode 7 ('No Stars for Naughty Boys')

CONTESTANT: Lolly Adefope

TIME: 23 minutes

METHODOLOGY: Lolly wedged herself in the shower cubicle in the toilet, behind a plank. Alex looked for her in the bathroom twice and didn't see her – at one point pretending that the task had finished to trick her into coming out. Lolly also called Alex to taunt him, sending him multiple photos of herself 'hiding' (at the beach and as a baby).

SCORE: 5

RELEVANT QUOTE: 'That's going to baffle him. You've hidden yourself in time!' – Greg Davies

Longest and best task attempt, no. 3

TASK: Stick your tongue out. The tongue that sticks out for the longest wins

EPISODE: Series 13, episode 8 ('You Tuper Super')

CONTESTANT: Sophie Duker

TIME: 26 minutes, 20 seconds

METHODOLOGY: Sophie was made to lick a lemon, then sherbert, then an ice lolly whenever Alex blew his whistle, and then stick her tongue out in front of a fan whenever Alex honked his horn. Despite angry muffled complaints (and Alex constantly telling her

5 / AN ORDERLY SPECIES

that she could stop at any time), Sophie kept her tongue out until the ice lolly was completely gone.

SCORE: 5

RELEVANT QUOTE: 'I don't think I know who I am if I'm not licking those things any more.' – Sophie Duker

Longest and worst task attempt, no. 1

TASK: Find out what this gentleman did for a living

EPISODE: Series 3, episode 4 ('A Very Nuanced Character')

CONTESTANT: Paul Chowdhry

TIME: 42 minutes, 7 seconds

METHODOLOGY: Paul got that the gentleman was a doctor relatively quickly, but was then infuriated to learn that he had to narrow that down ('For f***'s sake you f***ing bastard'). He said 'doctor' another 63 times, as well as swearing 23 times and making 15 sexual references. Eventually he got that the man was an anaesthetist but forgot what the word for anaesthetist was.

OTHER THINGS PAUL GUESSED: Bum doctor, yoga instructor, rent boy, babysitter, hygiene doctor, Dr. Dre

SCORE: 1, deservedly

RELEVANT QUOTES: 'Did you ever get involved with the nurses?' – Paul at his lowest ebb with the doctor

Longest and worst task attempt, no. 2

TASK: Retrieve a ping pong ball from a tube without moving the tube

EPISODE: Series 5, episode 3 ('Phoenix')

CONTESTANT: Nish Kumar

TIME: 44 minutes, 22 seconds

METHODOLOGY: After asking Alex if this was a 'sucking task', Nish attempted to block some of the holes in the tube with paper. This didn't work, but he kept trying it anyway (the Nish Kumar way). He then switched to clingfilm in the belief that it was waterproof (it was not). Eventually he cobbled together enough stoppers to just about get the water level high enough to allow everyone to get on with their lives.

SCORE: Amazingly, 2 (Aisling Bea was disqualified)

RELEVANT QUOTES: 'God it's like a bassoon!' – Nish after 30 minutes (reportedly)

Longest and worst task attempt, no. 3

TASK: Solve the riddle

EPISODE: Series 12, episode 4 ('The Customised Inhaler')

CONTESTANTS: Desiree Burch, Guz Khan and Morgana Robinson

TIME: 93 minutes

METHODOLOGY: The task was to solve a riddle consisting of various clues in the different rooms the contestants were in. The problem was that many of the most important clues were in the lab, where Guz Khan was, and Guz was more interested in writing a song called 'This Task Is Shit'. Desiree Burch attempted in vain to fumble her way to a solution, while Guz occasionally leapt on the walkie-talkie to breathlessly tell everyone, 'There's been another revelation in the lab.' In the end the answer to the riddle was 'nothing' – a typically colossal waste of everyone's time.

5 / AN ORDERLY SPECIES

SCORE: An overly generous 2

RELEVANT QUOTES: 'There's been another revelation in the lab!' – Guz Khan every five minutes; 'F*** me in the face.' – Desiree Burch after one revelation too many

Longest and worst task attempt EVER

TASK: Get this duck into that pond

EPISODE: Champion of Champions 2 ('The Alpine Darling')

CONTESTANT: Ed Gamble

TIME: 97 minutes

METHODOLOGY: Ed attempted to create a river for the rubber duck to sail down using drainpipes. He started quickly ('Other people might do something similar so I'm running!') and got the duck about halfway down the drainpipe, but ultimately the slope of the river was too gentle to create enough momentum for the duck to go down and the structure itself was so unstable that it was prone to frequent breakdowns (much like Ed). Despite this, he channeled his inner Nish, refusing to change his approach. He became angrier and angrier, sawing away at drainpipes, kicking rubber bricks, swearing at Alex when he dared to wish him good luck. The duck eventually got stuck in a pipe and that was the final straw. Ed grabbed the duck, sawed off its head, dug two holes in the back garden and buried the head in one and the body in another. A glorious, historic failure.

SCORE: Inexplicably, he somehow avoided a disqualification (Greg possibly didn't want to end up beheaded in the back garden)

RELEVANT QUOTE: 'The only way I get out of this with any dignity is if I die right now.' – Ed Gamble

OTHER IMPORTANT, SURPRISINGLY LONG TIMES IN THE SHOW

🦆 247,680 minutes (and counting): Frankie Boyle's time to (not) complete the 'Unwind this ball of string' task, when he failed to see the back of the card and read the second part of the task, 'Put a neat ball of string on the cushion.'

🦆 22 minutes, 47 seconds: The longest time anyone has ever spent on a task that they were then disqualified for – Paul Sinha spent that long failing to disguise himself in a phone box in series 8.

🦆 2 hours, 57 minutes: How long Desiree Burch took to burst the balloon in the portcullis (if you add up all the balloon-popping implements she purchased with 'time').

🦆 15 minutes: The amount of time Tim Vine spent crawling through a child's play tunnel, for no reason, before opening the 'Work out how long the piece of string is' task.

🦆 6 minutes: The length of time it took Mark Watson to open a briefcase to get a task (the code was 0000 and the briefcase was on 0000 at the start of filming).

🦆 11 minutes: The amount of time Sally Phillips spent shaving a coconut.

5 / AN ORDERLY SPECIES

Edinburgh Task 4: How Did It Go?

That advent my postman had to hand over fifteen copies of Eddie Large's autobiography, some signed by Eddie Large himself (and ten from one competitor, Steve Hall), and two huge rolls of bubblewrap from both Dan Atkinson and Stu Goldsmith (which I had to pop in order to transport to the Edinburgh show). But most notable was a letter which arrived (with a wooden plate) from the Post Office, thanks to Mike Wozniak, on 20 December. It read:

To whom it may concern, this plinth has been repackaged and sent on to the intended address in line with Post Office protocol. On receipt the original package was noted as containing the following: one circular acacia wood plinth – 25cm diameter – upon which rests one ice sculpture of a giant one-legged man standing on tiptoe and carrying a giant winged horse, also on tiptoe. Sculpture dimensions: 40 metres height, 16 metres width, approximately. Sent by Michael Wozniak of London. It is suspected that the item was larger than described above at the time of sending. This is evidenced by the fact that the horse's ears were disproportionately small and were dripping. Following receipt the item suffered catastrophic melt diminishment owing to a storage error. The Post Office accepts full responsibility for this as the sender clearly sent the item in good faith and at a time of cold weather. As an aside, it is worth noting that this is the single largest item myself or any of my colleagues have witnessed being sent in the history of the Post Office.

EDINBURGH TASK 5
4 January 2010

Dear All,

Happy New Year and many thanks for the large gifts that arrived at my house throughout December. The bar has most certainly been raised. Some truly remarkable performances. I just need to check a couple of things before revealing the results — the most pressing being: who sent me the 2.3 metre-high inflatable beanstalk elephant pool, and who sent me the large flat cardboard box that once contained a mirror and had to be opened in a special way?

Now on to the first of this year's challenges. In respect of the hard work you all put in last month, this one's far briefer:

BUMPER BOY: HOW MUCH WILL IT COST ME TO GET MY WIFE'S CAR FIXED?

On the night before New Year's Eve I drove my wife's beloved red Renault off a very high curb and this month I have to get it mended. Please find photos of damage attached. I'm planning on taking the broken vehicle to a Renault garage this month — how much do you think they'll charge me to make it better?

That's it. It's a mechanic's sort of question really. Nothing fancy. A guessing game. Good luck. If you happen to know someone who'll fix it cheaply, that'd be great, of course. But really, it's just a matter of guessing how much it will cost me to get my wife's car fixed.

BUT THERE ARE TWO OTHER ONGOING CHALLENGES YOU SHOULD BE AWARE OF:

1. JOHN SCALES: You sent me your weights. Thank you. Now that I know how much you currently weigh, the five people who INCREASE their weight by the most come August (and Edinburgh) will receive points (10 to the winner, 8 to the second etc). (Mr Wrigglesworth, by the way, is in the unfortunate position of weighing 12.85 stone.)

2. SPORTS RELIEF: The current leader, Mr Wehn, and I played a game of golf in December. At stake were 4 points. If he won, he'd have gained 4 points. But if he lost, he'd lose 4 of the points he'd already won. He lost. Hence his lead has been diminished, as you will see when the new league table is published in the next couple of days. If you too would like to challenge me at a sport — any sport (except long distance running and deep sea diving), name the place, the date, how many points you'd like to barter for (10 maximum), and I'll do my best to accommodate you.

Thanks again.

Yours,

The Taskmaster

6

I'VE SINNED AGAIN

TASKMASTER AND LAW AND ORDER

Crime. Nowhere is safe from it, not even the Taskmaster house. Over the course of seventeen series, there have been pasta robbers, Anne Boleyn murderers and gold pen thieves (we will catch you one day, Kiell Smith-Bynoe). It's time to name and shame them all, and show that there is a consequence for lying (disqualification), cheating (disqualification) and being mean to Alex Horne (bonus points).

TASKMASTER RULES

You must not discuss any of the tasks with your fellow competitors.

You must not break the law.

The Taskmaster's word is final

TASKMASTER RULES

A HISTORY OF CHEATING

As we all know from Sarah Kendall, it's fun to follow the rules. But there are some awful people out there who, for some reason or another, think it's cool to lie and cheat on the show, to turn the pure innocent Taskmaster house into a den of sin. May the Lord Greg Davies have mercy on the following contestants' souls.

Tim Key

NICKNAME: The Bathtub Fiddler

EPISODE: Series 1, episode 1 ('Melon Buffet')

TASK: Completely empty this bathtub without removing the plug

THEIR CRIME: During a particularly vigorous attempt at this task where he was shovelling water out of the bath with his bare hands, Tim pulled the plug loose, therefore breaking the rules of the task.

THE DEFENCE: Tim said it was an accident, and yet footage showed him putting the plug back in the bath in an attempt to cover up his crime.

ADMISSION OF GUILT: Initially Tim tried to deny the cover up, claiming that what looked like him putting the plug back into the bath was just him 'having a little walk around,' but he soon gave up: 'I picked the plug up, mate, and then put it back in the bath secretly.'

THE VERDICT: Greg put him in last place, although technically he should have been disqualified for unplugging the bath, regardless of the cover-up.

RELEVANT QUOTES: 'Tim, will you cheat again?' – Greg Davies. 'Yes.' – Tim Key

Dave Gorman

NICKNAME: The Pea Taker

EPISODE: Series 3, episode 1 ('A Pea in a Haystack')

TASK: Propel this pea the furthest and land it on the red carpet

THEIR CRIME: Dave lost the pea that he was tasked with using by flicking it with a tennis racket into the grass. He then asked Alex to get him a frozen pea (not to use, but to have as 'a snack'). Within seconds of receiving the new pea, Dave claimed that he had found the original pea within the strings of the racket. According to him, it must have got wedged in there when he flicked the pea. Of course.

THE DEFENCE: When he was shown footage of his original flick – where it was clear that the pea didn't lodge itself in the racket – he then claimed that it must have got caught up in the racket while he was using it to sweep through the grass. At this point Rob Beckett told him to, 'Turn it in, mate.'

ADMISSION OF GUILT: Dave Gorman was asked twice if he cheated by Greg (while insisting that 'you're not in trouble'). Both times he said no.

THE VERDICT: After watching all five attempts, Greg disqualified Dave, but did say he admired him for having a go.

RELEVANT QUOTE: 'I believe him. I believe Dave.' – Al Murray, inexplicably

6 / I'VE SINNED AGAIN

Dave Gorman (again)

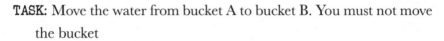

NICKNAME: The Tea Splosher

EPISODE: Series 3, episode 5 ('The F.I.P.')

TASK: Move the water from bucket A to bucket B. You must not move the bucket

THEIR CRIME: After trying at first to use a colander (with sellotape over the holes), he resorted to using the hose, sucking up the water in bucket A and then dropping it in bucket B. Despite his struggles, he somehow managed to post a score of 7.8cm, the second highest score of the round (after Al Murray, who paid Alex to move the buckets for him). It was only afterwards that the audience saw the actual liquid in bucket B: a lot of tea, which Dave happened to be drinking at the time.

THEIR DEFENCE: When Sara Pascoe asked him why the liquid in the bucket was tea-coloured, Dave claimed that the liquid he was moving from bucket A was poisonous and that meant he was bringing up bile from within him. He also claimed that he wasn't in good shape and the whole thing was making him feel quite nauseous.

ADMISSION OF GUILT: When Greg asked if he had cheated, Dave replied, 'Might have done.' Once the footage of the tea-dropping was shown, Dave tried to get out of trouble by offering to give money to a dolphin charity.

THE VERDICT: Disqualification, this time with no admiration from Greg.

RELEVANT QUOTES: 'Have you again cheated?' – Greg Davies. 'I can honestly say no to that, because I didn't cheat before.' – Dave Gorman

Noel Fielding

NICKNAME: The Clock Tamperer

EPISODE: Series 4, episode 2 ('Look At Me')

TEAM TASK: Land the flour on the target. You may not leave the bandstand

THEIR CRIME: The team of three got more flour on the bandstand, after chucking balls of wet flour at the target (which Alex then dried with his bunsen), but it was revealed after the task that they had recieved extra time, because Noel had meddled with Alex's clock.

THEIR DEFENCE: Noel defensively asked if Alex had any proof of the alleged clock-tampering. He did, because the show is televised, so there are a lot of cameras filming the contestants.

ADMISSION OF GUILT: Noel claimed he didn't do it, but went all silent once the footage was slowed down and zoomed in to show him fiddling with the clock.

THE VERDICT: All the team's points were taken away (just for that task, not for the entire show, as Joe thought originally).

RELEVANT QUOTES: 'What don't we countenance on this show?' – Greg Davies. 'Dancing. Sorry, cheating.' – Alex Horne

6 / I'VE SINNED AGAIN

Mawaan Rizwan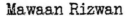

NICKNAME: The Sneaky Pasta Snake

EPISODE: Series 10, episode 3 ('Point of Swivel')

TASK: Put all the spaghetti into the grapefruit

THEIR CRIME: At the end of this task (the last two minutes of which were done in total darkness), the spaghetti jar was empty and Mawaan claimed he had managed to get the whole one kilogram of spaghetti into the grapefruit. Alex wasn't so sure and, after hearing some 'noises' as Mawaan left the room, he later checked Mawaan's dressing room to discover a mound of uncooked spaghetti in his bin, which Mawaan had hidden in his clothes during the period of darkness.

THEIR DEFENCE: Mawaan claimed at first that this was a stitch-up, but when the rest of the contestants turned on him, he argued that it wasn't his fault: 'You put me in the dark and I'm gonna have some fun.'

ADMISSION OF GUILT: Greg gave Mawaan the opportunity to stand in front of everyone and admit that he was a sneaky pasta snake. Mawaan at first rejected this ('Once you've been labelled a sneaky pasta snake, that's it, innit.'), but then agreed that, for the crucial four minutes of the task, he was a sneaky pasta snake.

THE VERDICT: Mawaan's cheating didn't actually impact his score as Alex judged this task by how much pasta was in the grapefruit, not how little was left in the jar. Even with the admission of the pasta-snake-sneakiness, Greg allowed Mawaan to take a deserved 4 points.

RELEVANT QUOTES: 'I still get paid, right?' – Mawaan Rizwan, faced with the threat of being disqualified from the whole show

Munya Chawawa

NICKNAME: The Bernard Basher

EPISODE: Series 14, episode 7 ('The System of Endless Plates')

TASK: Make an exercise ball touch Bernard. You may not touch any balls after each launch. Most balls actively involved in a successful launch wins

THEIR CRIME: Munya set up Alex as a human shield to spoon the balls into Bernard's direction and it looked initially as if he had created a perfect system, hitting as many as fifteen balls before banging into Bernard. However, a second look at the attempt showed Munya giving one of the balls a deliberate kick to send it on its way, which was clearly against the rules.

THEIR DEFENCE: He didn't say anything as the cheating footage made it very clear: he had been caught, bang to rights.

ADMISSION OF GUILT: No admission of guilt in the footage, but a rather incriminating 'What you don't know can't hurt you' as he walked away.

THE VERDICT: Instant disqualification.

RELEVANT QUOTES: 'I don't know what to believe any more.' – Greg Davies, having had his faith in humanity shattered

6 / I'VE SINNED AGAIN

Joe Wilkinson

NICKNAME: The Potato King

EPISODE: Series 2, episode 1 ('Fear of Failure')

TASK: Get a potato into the hole without touching the red green

THEIR CRIME: Joe threw the potato into the hole on his first attempt, after six seconds, but it was revealed afterwards that Joe had, deliberately, and with great malice and forethought, completely unambiguously trodden on the red green to gain an unfair advantage.

THEIR DEFENCE: Joe had none, but he begged for leniency, literally getting down on his knees and murmuring, 'Please don't take it away from me' to Greg.

THE VERDICT: After sending Joe out of the room, Greg asked the cheater's fellow contestants what he should do. They rightly said he should be disqualified.

RELEVANT QUOTES: 'Guys, sometimes it's hard to be the Taskmaster. Sometimes you gotta crush dreams.' – Greg Davies

FACTS ABOUT EGGS 2

🥚 Did you know that, according to a ruling by the Taskmaster in series 9, the definition of an egg does NOT include the eggshell?

🥚 In a task where the contestants had to get whole eggs into a variety of metal things, and where they had to release their eggs while on the chair, David Baddiel chose destruction both of eggs and of the entire concept of the English language. He broke the egg into a baking tray while sitting on the chair (claiming that this was 'releasing' the egg), and then walked over to a vat, into which he poured the egg.

🥚 In the studio, Greg countered that the shell is part of the egg so the act of breaking it was not 'releasing' it. David looked dumbfounded (fairly standard for him in the show), before he got support from an unlikely source, Little Alex Horne, who stated that, according to the dictionary, 'the eggs of birds are enclosed in a chalky shell,' implying that eggs are the thing *inside* the shell. Greg ate his words and awarded David 3 points.

🥚 Susie Dent, on the *Taskmaster Podcast*, pointed out that the ramifications of defining an egg in such a way are wide-reaching: any contestant who has been disqualified for a 'broken' egg could surely now appeal against the decision, throwing the entire *Taskmaster* scoring system into disarray. Which for 3 points seems a bit much.

MOST CONTESTED TASKS

No-one likes an argument. Except Alex Horne, who created an entire television format to get his comedian friends to argue on primetime TV. Here are some of the biggest arguments and debates on the show, angry enough to make even the mildest-mannered ex-*Inbetweeners* star lose their cool.

High-five a 55-year-old.

EPISODE: Series 1, episode 2 ('The Pie Whisperer')

CRUX OF THE ARGUMENT: Can you use false claims of being on Comic Relief to complete a task?

DEFENDANT: Tim Key

PLAINTIFFS: Romesh Ranganathan, Roisin Conaty

KEY POINTS: Tim achieved his high-five by, in a moment of madness, telling the person he wanted to high-five that he was doing it for Comic Relief. While everyone in the audience applauded his audacity, Romesh told him he should be ashamed of himself.

LEGAL COUNSEL: Surprisingly, Josh Widdicombe came to Tim's defence, arguing that the card didn't specify that you shouldn't use charity as a lie (although as Greg pointed out it didn't specify not to punch an old woman in the face either).

VERDICT: Initially Greg allowed Tim to keep his original position of second, as long as he donated a certain amount of money to Comic Relief (Alex specified £185, because it feels right – not too much but quite a lot of money), but when Tim started to bid for first place, Greg dropped him down to third anyway.

RELEVANT QUOTES: 'I think I'll buy first. What was it, twelve-and-a-half grand? I've probably got that on me.' – Frank Skinner, when Tim started trying to buy his way to first place; 'I feel like we're choosing who's going to host the next World Cup.' – Josh Widdicombe

Fill an egg cup with your sweat.

EPISODE: Series 3, episode 3 ('Little Polythene Grief Cave')

CRUX OF THE ARGUMENT: Is urine chemically the same as sweat?

DEFENDANT: Al Murray

PLAINTIFF: Every single other person on the planet

KEY POINTS: In an all-round disgusting task, where Paul Chowdhry's sweat was inexplicably brown and Rob Beckett had an individual task to speak in a hideous accent, Al Murray took the biscuit by deciding that, medically, sweat and urine are the same thing. He went into the toilet, urinated into a pan and poured it into the egg cup. It was unpleasant.

LEGAL EXPERTISE: Alex consulted two expert witnesses (the van Tulleken twin doctors from the telly), who said that while sweat and urine are both mostly water, they are made in different ways, by a different part of the body, and are easy to distinguish, without the need for a scientific test. They finished by saying 'He's talking gibberish.'

VERDICT: Al protested that Google told him urine and sweat were the same thing. In a rare venture into satire, Greg told him that he'd allow Al to win if Google paid their taxes. Al was disqualified.

6 / I'VE SINNED AGAIN

RELEVANT QUOTE: 'God I thought *I* did the grossest thing possible in that challenge.' – Sara Pascoe, who paid men for their sweat

Completely erase this eraser.

EPISODE: Series 8, episode 10 ('Clumpy Swayey Clumsy Man')

CRUX OF THE ARGUMENT: Is an eraser erased if you chuck it in a hedge or flush it down the toilet?

DEFENDANTS: Sian Gibson, Iain Stirling, Paul Sinha, Lou Sanders

PLAINTIFF: Joe Thomas

KEY POINTS: While Joe Thomas obliterated the eraser by erasing it on sandpaper (Greg admired his technique), everyone else just chucked it somewhere ungettable. Sian tried to burn it, then threw it into a hedge, while Paul and Iain both flushed it down the toilet (with Paul claiming that he had 'removed it from society'). Lou, in classic Lou fashion, tried to eat it and then spat it into the toilet.

LEGAL EXPERTISE/PURE WHITE-HOT RAGE: Joe argued that while Sian, Paul and Iain had thrown their erasers away, they could still function as erasers if you went through the trouble of getting them out of the UK's creaking sewage system. When Iain tried to argue back, the usually calm Joe blew up: 'I'm so fed up of putting in loads of genuine physical effort into the task and then these other people find some wanky workaround.'

VERDICT: When wise heads needed to prevail, the Taskmaster provided his. He gave points based on speed (as the task stated), but then gave three bonus points to Joe for his dedication to the concept of erasing, and an extra bonus point to Lou for being weird and trying to eat an eraser.

RELEVANT QUOTE: 'Put some f***ing effort in.' – Joe Thomas, to his fellow non-erasing contestants; 'Where the f*** has this come from?' – a hurt Iain Stirling

Strike the most drumskins and cymbals with a single throw of a bouncy ball

EPISODE: Series 15, episode 5 ('Old Honkfoot')

CRUX OF THE ARGUMENT: Should tying a ball to a piece of cord and jerking it around count as a single throw?

DEFENDANT: Mae Martin

PLAINTIFFS: Frankie Boyle, Ivo Graham, Jenny Eclair, Kiell Smith-Bynoe, the studio audience

KEY POINTS: While other contestants painstakingly took apart a drum kit and then came up with elaborate ways to guide the ball to hit as many drum skins as possible, Mae Martin came up with a sneaky workaround. They tied a ball to a piece of string and then dangled it across the drumkit, hitting as many skins as they could, claiming that the initial drop of the dangling ball was the 'single throw' and that all subsequent hits should count as part of it. They looked very pleased with themselves, but back in the studio the audience were nonplussed; does that count as a single throw?

LEGAL EXPERTISE: Frankie Boyle went for the fairground argument that if you had a single throw to knock over a coconut and instead tied a piece of string to it and swung it around until it knocked one off, you might get a beating. All four other contestants got involved in the litigation: Kiell claimed it was a drop; Frankie said it was a cast; Jenny complained it was supposed to be percussion, not strings and percussion; while Ivo disputed the difference between a jerk and a throw ('I don't throw my penis across the room every morning, do I?').

VERDICT: Frankie's interjection that it was a 'cast' may have been crucial, because when Alex looked it up he discovered that a cast is categorised as a type of throw (leading Frankie to say, 'That's clearly where I've been going wrong with fishing, I should be throwing the f***ing rod'). In the end Greg's decision was final. He let Mae get away with it, earning them 5 points, and the message boards have been raging ever since.

RELEVANT QUOTE: 'This is my favourite thing, ever.' – Alex Horne, on making all the contestants fight; 'You know the thing that's swinging it in your favour the most?' – Greg Davies; 'Is it swinging it or throwing it?' – Ivo Graham

MOST DISQUALIFIED CONTESTANTS

9 Iain Stirling (series 8)
    Katherine Parkinson (series 10)
    Ivo Graham (series 15)

8 Johnny Vegas (series 10)
    Mawaan Rizwan (series 10)
    Sue Perkins (series 16)

7 Joe Wilkinson (series 2)
    Phil Wang (series 7)
    Rhod Gilbert (series 7)
    Frankie Boyle (series 15)
    Kiell Smith-Bynoe (series 15)
    Mae Martin (series 15)

LEAST DISQUALIFIED CONTESTANTS

0 Ed Gamble (series 9) (the big swot)

A BRIEF HISTORY OF TWO-PART TASKS: A LESSON IN CONSEQUENCES

There are five words that every *Taskmaster* contestant dreads hearing at the end of the task 'Can I give you this?' These words, accompanied by Alex handing over another task, are enough to turn elation and relief into out-and-out despair, because it means that there is a fresh horror to discover. Here are five of the most influential two-part tasks in the history of the show.

EPISODE: Series 4, episode 8 ('Tony Three Pies')

TASK 1: Make the most exotic sandwich

NOTABLE ATTEMPTS: Mel Giedroyc created a nine-layer sweet sandwich with Turkish Delight, Crunchie, Twix and Snickers, and a marshmallow topping. Joe Lycett created 'The Mothers' Delight' (Arctic Roll, uncooked yam and smoked trout). Noel Fielding put Alex between two slices of bread and made him dance exotically.

TASK 2: Eat your exotic sandwich

NOTABLE ATTEMPTS: Mel Giedroyc turned her giant sandwich on its side like an accordion and tried to unhinge her jaw to stuff it in, accidentally snorting a blue M&M in the process. Lolly Adefope ate a surprising amount of her 'prawns and frankfurter' sandwich. Noel Fielding ate part of Alex's beard. It was horrific.

WHY IT IS IMPORTANT? The original – and arguably the best – two-parter taught contestants a valuable lesson: that like some kind of Greek tragedy, the horrors they birthed on this show could be turned against them to ruin them.

WINNER: No one. Everyone received the exact same number of points for the combined tasks, except Mel and Noel, who received bonus points for snorting an M&M and eating Alex's beard respectively.

RELEVANT QUOTES: 'Oh gang' – Mel Giedroyc on discovering the second task; 'It's not that kind of show.' – Noel Fielding on discovering the second task (and that he would have to eat Alex)

EPISODE: Series 7, episode 10 ('I Can Hear it Gooping.')

TASK 1: When you hear this siren, put on a boiler suit and lie flat on the ground

TASK 2: Tie yourself up as securely as possible. (The siren from task 1 goes off midway through this task.)

NOTABLE ATTEMPTS: James Acaster tied his feet up first, so that when the siren went off he had to hop through the garden, swearing at Alex the whole time. Kerry Godliman had, in Greg's words, a 'full on kid's hissy fit on the floor' when she had to abandon her tying to put on the boiler suit. Due to his own incompetence, Phil Wang had failed to tie himself up when the siren went off so was perfectly placed to do the boiler suit task. Rhod Gilbert was midway through tying up Alex (as part of his series-long campaign to bully the assistant at every opportunity), so he had no trouble putting on the boiler suit.

WHY IT IS IMPORTANT? This was the first time a task at the start of the episode/filming day was left unresolved, so that its conclusion could completely torpedo the contestants in the middle of another task. It also showed how two-part tasks are the great equalisers. Being good at the first part will make the second part that much harder, and vice versa.

6 / I'VE SINNED AGAIN

WINNER: Rhod Gilbert, because Alex never actually got out of the bind

RELEVANT QUOTES: 'You piece of shit, Alex. This is the worst one so far. This is the worst day of my life.' – James Acaster; 'That was the moment where I remembered that my agent told me this would be a good career opportunity.' – Jessica Knappett on writhing about on the floor putting on the boiler suit

EPISODE: Series 9, episode 3 ('Five Miles a Day')

TASK 1: Build the most robust statue of the most delicate thing

NOTABLE ATTEMPTS: David Baddiel created a physical representation of his battered ego as a fourteen-year-old after he had been rejected by a Scottish girl called Avril Cowan (who responded to his request for a date with 'Oh I wish you hadn't asked me that.') Jo Brand made a statue of herself and then attempted to convince the Taskmaster that she was delicate and liked poetry. Rose Matafeo and Katy Wix both did leaves, although only Rose managed to accidentally nail hers to a table. Ed Gamble made a baby, disturbingly complete with nipples.

TASK 2: Score a goal with this steamroller, using your statue as a goalkeeper

NOTABLE ATTEMPTS: David Baddiel struggled to control the steamroller, frequently losing track of the football, accidentally crushing Avril without even scoring (again). Jo Brand flattened herself in eight minutes, in an action that Greg described as 'genuinely heartbreaking'. Ed crushed his baby with little remorse, murmuring just before he did it, 'I think we all know what's going to happen now, don't we?'

AN ABSOLUTE CASSEROLE

WHY IT IS IMPORTANT? It's a metaphor for the creative industry: turning your most delicate ideas into something robust that you can take pride in, all the while knowing that you will likely have to flatten it into something unrecognisable if you want to attain success. Or it's just a fun silly task. I dunno.

WINNER: Rose Matafeo (4 points for the statue, 5 points for the goal)

RELEVANT QUOTES: 'I mean if I'd known in advance, I wouldn't have made a baby.' – Ed Gamble; 'What is THAT?!' – Rose Matafeo, about her own statue (pre-squishing)

EPISODE: Series 14, episode 9 ('A New Business End')

TASK 1: Write a one-minute, one-person play

TASK 2: Stage and perform another contestant's one minute, one person play

NOTABLE ATTEMPTS: Fern Brady performed Sarah Millican's 'The Not Cat Café', a mournful story about Sarah's fading relationship with her nana and her cat who was always mean to Sarah. With ping pong balls attached to her glasses, Sarah Millican performed Munya Chawawa's 'The Power of Silence', a play that was, in her words, the sort of thing she'd avoid at the Edinburgh Fringe. John Kearns performed Dara Ó Briain's play 'Every Time I Look Up I Think Of You', the harrowing tale of an astronaut going to Mars, who discovers only at the end of the countdown that his wife at ground control has sabotaged his navigation system as revenge for his infidelity. Dara Ó Briain performed John Kearns's ten-word play 'Door(s)', which was about doors. Presumably.

THE ED GAMBLLERY

Over seventeen series, there have been some incredible works of art – far too many to feature here. So we've asked series 9 champion, host of the *Taskmaster* podcast, and walking work of triple-denim art Ed Gamble to curate a gallery made up of the best pictures in *Taskmaster* history.

Horse, Frank Skinner, 2015
Horse motion, poster paint on paper

Task: 'Paint the best picture of a horse whilst riding a horse.'
(series 1, episode 1)

Self Portrait,
Paul Chowdhry, 2016

Mustard, brown sauce, ketchup, burger sauce, squirty cream, wall

Task: 'Create the best upside-down self-portrait using only the materials supplied. The Taskmaster will judge the picture rotated by 180 degrees.' (series 3, episode 2)

Taskmaster, A Sexual Gladiator,
Noel Fielding, 2017

Paint, canvas (on red green, 6 foot away from artist)

Task: 'Paint the best picture of the Taskmaster. Only the paint and brush may touch the mat, easel and canvas. You have 10 minutes.' (series 4, episode 2)

***The Leprechauns Do Be Hanging Out**, Aisling Bea*
Scented paints, canvas (painted in total darkness)

Task: 'Paint the best rainbow scene. You may not open the lab door until the task is complete.' (series 5, episode 2)

***Her Majesty the Cream**, Tim Vine, 2018*
Squirty cream, floor

Task: 'Make the best art using the entire contents of this can of squirty cream.' (series 6, episode 6)

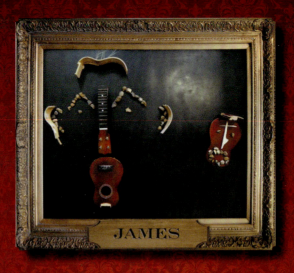

The Fear in Alex's Face, James Acaster, 2018
49 pebbles and a ukelele

Task: 'Put exactly 50 different things in this bin. Make the best picture of the Taskmaster using all 50 items.' (series 7, episode 6)

Romesh Ranganathan, Paul Sinha, 2019
Barbecue blower, sand

Task: 'Make the best picture in the sand of a former *Taskmaster* contestant. You must roll the dice to choose your implement. Nothing but air may touch the sand at any point.' (series 8, episode 8)

Tiny Bit of Bollock, David Baddiel, 2019

Pen on flipchart

Task: 'Draw a portrait of the Taskmaster using 16 A1 pages. You may not remove the A1 pages from the flipchart during your drawing. After the task the A1 pages will be laid out in the pattern shown on the front page.' (series 9, episode 2)

The Taskmaster's Lovely Irises, Daisy May Cooper, 2020

Balloon, peg, cape, shoes (artist's own)

Task: 'Make the best portrait of the Taskmaster and his favourite toy using only balloons, pegs, and your own clothes.' (series 10 episode 2)

Epic, Charlotte Ritchie, Jamali Maddix, Sarah Kendall, 2021
Poster paint, spray paint, wall

Task: 'Vandalise this wall. Most creative vandalism wins.'
(series 11, episode 6)

I Don't Know if My Self-Esteem Is Going to Survive This Series, Victoria Coren Mitchell, 2021
Paint, 'big pencils', 'just a stick', canvas (six feet above artist's head)

Task: 'Paint the most flattering picture of the Taskmaster in action. You must lie flat on your back on the creeper at all times. You must tell Alex if you want the canvas to be six inches or six feet above you within the next ten seconds.'
(series 12, episode 1)

Taskmaster, Chris Ramsey, 2022
Lips, lipstick

Task: 'Create the best picture of the Taskmaster using only lipstick on your lips.' (series 13, episode 1)

Horse/A Series of Lines, John Kearns, 2022
Paint, 6-foot-long brush

Task: 'Paint a picture of a horse using your head brush.' (series 14, episode 6)

The Taskmaster (after Munch's *The Scream*),
Sam Campbell, 2023
Biro on Post-it

Task: 'Recreate a well-known piece of art on these memo squares. You may only look at one memo square at a time.' (series 16, episode 4)

6 / I'VE SINNED AGAIN

WHY IT IS IMPORTANT? This was the first time the contestants' tasks interacted with one another, in the sense that they were all writing plays for the others to perform before many of them had even met. As Fern Brady pointed out, she hadn't actually encountered Sarah Millican before the studio recordings, yet here she's being made to impersonate her (in a deeply autobiographical and moving monologue). It was a very risky double task that could have backfired, but it really worked. Except for Munya's, which was pretty rubbish.

RELEVANT QUOTES: 'Is there no dialogue? Oh you dick.' – Sarah Millican, reading Munya's play; 'My one-minute play was MUCH better than this.' – Dara Ó Briain, reading John's play; 'Howay man.' – Fern Brady as Sarah Millican

EPISODE: Series 16, episode 7 ('I'm Off To Find a Robin')

TASK 1: Do whatever you like with these switches for five minutes

TASK 2 Balance the most tees on the shelves in the lab, while dealing with the consequences of the switches you flicked during task 1

WHY IT WAS SO SNEAKY? None of the switches were labelled, so the contestants had no idea what they were switching on and off. As it turned out, the switches they flicked in task 1 made a bunch of stuff happen in task 2: they turned the lights out; they turned on a vibrating plate on which the contestants were standing; they caused a pile of leaves to fall from the ceiling and onto their attempt; they made a speaker play with someone saying their name over and over again.

NOTABLE ATTEMPTS: Sam Campbell had given himself a bit of time 'just to muck around', but ruined that by flicking all the switches at once, triggering leaves, vibration and sound (someone yelling 'Sam Campbell' at him). He balanced his tees on the physical task as a workaround. Julian Clary's vibration plate malfunctioned and wouldn't turn off, so he had to remain on the plate for a minute afterwards ('Get your thrills where you can at my age'). Susan Wokoma only realised halfway through that the best tactic was to flick none of the switches in the first half of the task.

WHY IT IS IMPORTANT? It's less a task and more an updated version of the Stanford marshmallow experiment: the aim in the first part should be to resist the urge to flick any switches, to make the second half of the task vaguely possible, but of course everyone fails to do exactly that. As Alex puts it, 'You've decided the conditions for this task. What happens in here is all your fault.' Like so many tasks in the show, it's about learning the consequences of one's actions.

RELEVANT QUOTES: 'Please don't make me fart in the dark listening to my own name.' – Sue Perkins, mid-breakdown in the lab, as all the switches go off at once; 'Don't like UV light very much. My mum thinks it was because I was in an incubator to help me grow.' – Lucy Beaumont, for no reason

TASKMASTER HALL OF GLORY

Lowest Score in an Episode

NAME: Mel Giedroyc

LOWEST SCORE IN AN EPISODE: 3 (0.5 points per task) (series 4, episode 3)

SERIES POINTS: 134 (2.98 points per task)

POSITION IN SERIES: Third (she managed to win three episodes despite this horror show)

FUN FACT: In this episode, Mel became the first contestant in the show's history to get minus points after not spotting the clause on the back of the task that outlined that eating the chocolate provided would be severely punished.

RELEVANT QUOTE: 'Mel's just going to have another little piece of choc.'

Edinburgh Task 5: How Did It Go?

These were frankly disappointing tasks that yielded little of interest. They were a good lesson that a purely mundane chore does not necessarily make for an entertaining task. As Dan Atkinson put it:

Dear Alex,

Seeing as you refuse to answer my quite reasonable questions about your bumper, it is only left for me to have a wild stab in the dark.

I have little mechanical training and even less knowledge of car maintenance.

Whoever does well at this task is a DICK who needs to GET A LIFE.

I think it will cost £278.31.

But I don't care.

Yours sincerely,

Dan

EDINBURGH TASK 6
4 February 2010

Morning all.

Here is the sixth task:

Please broadcast the following sentence to as many people as possible:

'ALEX HORNE IS A MAGNIFICENT MAN.'

Send me your evidence. The more people exposed to my magnificence the more points you receive.

Good luck.

In other news, I would like to apologise for the dullness of last month's car bumper task. Awful stuff. But thanks for those who grudgingly guessed.

I'm still updating the league table (I still don't know who sent me the enormous elephant paddling pool), but, just to assure you, it's tight.

Finally, if you'd like to challenge me to a sporting encounter for points, please do so. A number of you have and we haven't quite found the time to meet up yet, but the likes of darts, golf, table tennis, air hockey and unihockey on a unicycle are now taken ...

Bye!

NO STARS FOR NAUGHTY BOYS

TASKMASTER AND EDUCATION

Everyone at *Taskmaster* is a big fan of the three Rs (reading, writing and Rosalind). A wide array of subjects is tackled on the show – maths, history, art, the anatomy of Bob Mortimer's anus, and others. So strap on your mortarboard, get your PE kit on and do a couple of rounds of 'Punch the C***' – it's time to go back to school, *Taskmaster* style!

A HISTORY OF HACKS

School teaches us that there's no sacrifice for hard work and that true success cannot come through using easy shortcuts. But *Taskmaster* teaches us this is complete toshwash. In this game the way to win is to find the loopholes and exploit them mercilessly, like a ruthless coconut businessman. Here are some of the best hacks in *Taskmaster* history.

Identify the contents of these pies. You may touch the pies, but you may not breach their pastry.

EPISODE: Series 1, episode 2 ('The Pie Whisperer')

HACKER: Tim Key, Roisin Conaty

HACK: While Frank Skinner used a 'psychic approach' without much success – with Greg christening him the 'Pie Whisperer' – Tim and Roisin thought outside the box (or pie). Tim re-read the task and saw that while *he* couldn't breach the pastry, Alex could, so he got Alex to smash the pies with his fist. Roisin, meanwhile, got Alex to eat the pies, which was a great idea, ruined by an extra level of complication. In an attempt to say that she hadn't cheated, she faced the wall as Alex ate the pie and tried to guess the pie based on his reaction. Needless to say, Tim was more accurate.

PUSHBACK: A lot. While Frank was still getting his head round the concept of a toothpaste pie, Romesh Ranganthan and Josh Widdicombe fumed (which was pretty much all they did during the series). Greg was having none of it though. Tim was awarded the full 5 points.

7 / NO STARS FOR NAUGHTY BOYS

RELEVANT QUOTES: 'What is …what is even the point.' – Josh Widdicombe; 'I didn't know I could've just said, "Can you open the pies for me?"' – Frank Skinner; 'You don't look like you're having a nice time. And that makes me think that's not a nice-time pie.' – Roisin Conaty, trying to work out the contents of the toothpaste pie based on Alex's facial expressions

Silently make the tastiest cocktail with the best name. If you make a noise over 60dB, you must pour your cocktail into the bucket and shout your given phrase out at over 100dB.

EPISODE: Series 10, episode 6 ('Hippopotamus')

HACKER: Mawaan Rizwan

HACK: Every contestant struggled to clink ice and pour drinks into their glasses under 60dB and Mawaan was no exception. At one point he set off the sensor picking up a melon; at another he tried to use a crew member's jumper to muffle the sound of cocktail shaking without realising there were keys in the pocket, meaning he had to yell 'I'M SO SORRY' again. But then, inspiration struck. He realised that he could make a 'delicious' cocktail out of all the liquid he had thrown away into the bucket. He poured the worryingly beige fluid into a cocktail glass, popped a cocktail umbrella in and served it up to Alex. Bin Juice, à la Mawaan.

PUSHBACK: A fair amount from Alex, who tried to argue that the task stated '*tastiest* cocktail', and the combo of wine, milk, egg, orange, flecks of mud and an old hair was not tasty. He was quickly overruled by Greg (as per) and Mawaan took the 5 points.

RELEVANT QUOTES: 'I don't like how happy you are.' – Alex Horne watching Mawaan discover the loophole; 'Bin Juice: getting trashed!' – Mawaan Rizwan trying to sell the advertising campaign to Greg

Record the highest number on this pedometer.

EPISODE: Series 13, episode 6 ('The 75th Question')

HACKER: Bridget Christie

HACK: This was a hack that came less out of inspiration and more desperation. Try as she might, Bridget couldn't get her head around how a pedometer works and spent the majority of the task bounding over the garden with high knees, like the Childcatcher of the Wild West. With very few steps recorded, Bridget declared a new plan: she would sit down on the pedometer and record herself on her phone *saying* the biggest number she knew (which was eleven trillion gazillion, later downgraded to eleven trillion). Still, her attempt of 11,000,000,000,000 was just about enough to edge out Chris's 2,789.

PUSHBACK: Surprisingly little as most of the studio discussion was taken up by Bridget's technique for recording steps. Greg's first words were: 'It's not a question I expected to ask after this task, but have you ever walked, Bridget?'

RELEVANT QUOTES: 'I am stepping! But look! Step, step, step! Step! That is a step!' – Bridget Christie, trying to walk; 'It's very clever lateral thinking. But I would remind you of how she walks day to day, if it gives you a little lift.' – Greg Davies, trying to cheer up Judi Love after this task

Task Stage Three
Sausage Studies

The Study Guide

tten by the Taskmaster's Assistant

Sausage Facts

REMEMBER

The word sausage was first used in English in the mid-15th century, spelled sawsyge.

Typically, a sausage is formed in a casing traditionally made from intestines

The word sausage comes from the Latin word 'salsus' meaning salted.

The first ever vegetarian sausage had meat in it.

Did you know

Between July 2013 and July 2014, Britain consumed 181,853 tones of sausages, worth around £780million in retail sales.

The Greek poet Homer mentioned a kind of blood sausage in the Odyssey.

Queen Victoria loved a sausage, but insisted the meat was chopped rather than minced.

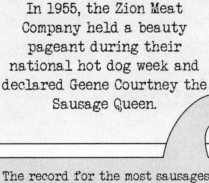

In 1955, the Zion Meat Company held a beauty pageant during their national hot dog week and declared Geene Courtney the Sausage Queen.

The record for the most sausages eaten in one minute is held by Leah Shutkever, from Birmingham. On 7th June 2020 she was able to eat 11 sausages in one minute. She broke her own record 21 days later by eating 12 in one minute.

The longest ever sausage was created in Romania at the end of 2014. It was a 38.99 miles long and weighed nearly 135kg.

In the UK the minimum meat content to be labelled 'pork sausages' is 42 per cent.

There are over 5,000 members in the British Sausage Appreciation Society.

Geene chopped 42 Australian intestines.

Sausage gambling has been practised in Taiwan since World War II.

Democracy Sausage was the Australian word of the year in 2016.

REMEMBER:

Always turn over the exam paper.

Geene chopped 42
Australian intestines.

STUPIDEST MOMENTS

There are many different ways to fail on *Taskmaster*. You can come up with a great ambitious plan that is thwarted by limitations outside your control. You can be scuppered by weather, the seasons, a sabotaging teammate or the structural integrity of boxes. Or you can suffer a massive brainfart right in the middle of a task which you then have to live with appearing on national television and, years later, in a tie-in book. This is a celebration of the four biggest brain blunders in the show's history.

4th place

IVO GRAHAM SITS FOR THREE MINUTES IN THE WRONG ROOM

TASK: Bingo – first to complete a line or four corners wins

MINI TASK: Sit in the shed for three minutes and think about what you've done

EPISODE: Series 15, episode 4 ('How Heavy is the Water?')

WHAT HAPPENED: In the task, Alex rolled a tombola and read out bingo numbers, and contestants had to do the corresponding task to the number to complete the line. In a rare moment of non-stupidity, Ivo decided against doing what every other contestant had done (immediately attempting the mini-task as it came to them) and instead obtained and opened every mini-task first, so that he could strategise the best tasks to complete. This was where the non-stupidity ended. As he laboured his way through the many tasks, declaring 'I'm having a bad time' as he did them, he reached the stage where completing *any* of the mini-tasks would get a bingo. Finally, having struggled throughout (including in a nightmare conversation with a person *not* called John), Ivo decided to go for the simplest but most time-consuming task: 'Sit in the shed for three minutes and think about what you've done.' Ivo sat in silence, his head in his hands, thinking about the many decisions that had led him there. It was only afterwards, when talking with Alex, that he realised he had sat in the caravan and not the shed.

STUDIO INTERROGATION: Greg decided against chit-chat and instead opted for the tragic image of Ivo, head in hands, in the not-shed. Ivo was too tired and sad to respond in any meaningful way.

POINTS: Unbelievably 2 – despite his shed-caravan anguish, he was just ahead of (future champion) Mae Martin.

RELEVANT QUOTES: 'It's gone terribly.' – Ivo Graham, upon leaving the caravan, about to discover that it had gone much worse

3rd place

KIELL SMITH-BYNOE IS TOO STUPID FOR THE STUPIDEST TASK

TASK: Do something really stupid

EPISODE: Champion of Champions 3

WHAT HAPPENED: Dressed as a terrible magician, Kiell demonstrated some terrible magic with a golf ball (much to Alex's mild horror), before putting Alex's hands through the spoke of a big wheel and getting him to hold two glasses with the words 'Alex's tears' written

7 / NO STARS FOR NAUGHTY BOYS

on them – the idea being that he couldn't release himself without spilling those tears. The problem was, Kiell had put Alex's arms through the wrong hole, so he could release himself fairly easily. As Alex said later in the studio, he was *genuinely* stupid.

STUDIO INTERROGATION: Greg tore into Kiell's performance, although he did also admit that when he said Kiell's task attempt out loud ('Hand Alex a bottle of his own tears through a wagon wheel') it was quite stupid.

POINTS: 1, because he was stupid by accident whereas everyone else was stupid in a thoughtful way, which seems a bit harsh to Kiell's boundless stupidity, but there you go.

RELEVANT QUOTE: 'I'm beginning to think that Mae Martin might take legal action against you.' – Greg Davies to Kiell, who was standing in for Mae Martin

2nd place

DAVID BADDIEL ADDS SPOONS TO A LASSO

TASK: Lasso Alex

EPISODE: Series 9, episode 5 ('Another Spoon')

WHAT HAPPENED: This task was supposed to be a tiebreaker, something quick and easy to decide an episode, and then David came along. He struggled to lasso Alex at first, but instead of trying to move the line he was behind, or throwing underarm, or asking Alex to come a little closer, he went off into the caravan and pulled out the well-known cowboy lasso tool: a wooden spoon. He tangled the rope around the spoon and tried again. No success. Undeterred, he went into the kitchen and got *yet more wooden spoons*, taping them to the lasso, before trying once more. At this stage he began to spin his unwieldy monstrosity around his torso, the 'lasso' (although it was more spoon than rope at this point) barely able to get off the ground as he spun it. The usually stoic Alex collapsed in giggles at the sight of one of the most famous comedians in Britain whirling a spoonasso, nearly taking out cameras and crew as he did so. Eventually he attached some kind of American football to the rope, stood on a step ladder, got Alex to kneel (not pray, he specified) and threw the rope just about over Alex's shoulder, before asking him to jiggle until the rope surrounded him. Yee haw.

STUDIO INTERROGATION: Greg was less interested in why David tried to add spoons in the first place and more why he *continued* to add spoons. Why not stop at two?

POINTS: This was the kind of stupid moment that lasts a lot, lot longer than a moment – twenty-four, to be precise. He took longer than everyone else combined, receiving 1 point.

RELEVANT QUOTE: 'I feel really bad about what I said about Katy now.' – Kerry Godliman, standing in for Katy Wix

1st place

KATHERINE PARKINSON CREATES A SPIDER

TASK: Put the wellies on the spider
EPISODE: Series 10, episode 10 ('Dog Meat Trifle')
CONTESTANT: Katherine Parkinson

7 / NO STARS FOR NAUGHTY BOYS

WHAT HAPPENED: This was a task that required contestants to take wellies from the lab and put them on a spider outside in the garden. But Katherine Parkinson has never been particularly good at leaving rooms on the show and this was no different. Looking around the room, she asked Alex, 'Where's the spider?' His response, that she would have to answer that for herself, was supposed to encourage independent thinking, but instead provoked a breakdown. 'There isn't a spider. Is that the spider? Am I the spider? Put these wellies on the spider's feet. What f***ing spider?' Then, suddenly, inspiration. 'Ahhhh. I know exactly what's going on,' she said, with the misplaced confidence of someone who absolutely doesn't. She then turned the table in the lab upside down, declared it to be a spider and put the eight wellies on the eight legs of the 'spider'. Alex stopped the clock. He had seen enough.

STUDIO INTERROGATION: Initially Greg tried to give her the benefit of the doubt. Sure, it might *look* like Katherine Parkinson had just put some wellies on some table legs, but maybe she had used artistic skill to *create* a spider out of table legs? After all, what is a spider? It was up to Daisy May Cooper to point out that a spider is a spider, not table legs.

POINTS: Inexplicably, 2, because Greg admired her thinking (and felt bad for being rude about the masks she made in lockdown).

RELEVANT QUOTE: 'Look, a cat!' – Mawaan Rizwan, holding up his own chair, 'creating' a new animal

GIVE ME SOME STATS:
Is it better to go to university?

Hypothesis

You have a better chance of success in *Taskmaster* if you went to university.

WHAT DO THE STATS SAY?
Categorically untrue: 67 out of the 85 contestants on the show attended university and those who did scored an average of 2.96 points per task. By contrast, the 18 contestants who didn't attend university scored 3.06 points per task and include champions Mae Martin, Morgana Robinson and Liza Tarbuck.

Out of the graduates, 16 contestants went to Oxford or Cambridge. While three of those contestants did win their series (with Richard Herring also winning Champion of Champions 2 and John Robins becoming the highest scoring contestant ever), it's worth saying that, on average, Oxbridge contestants do much, much worse than others, averaging just 2.90 points per task. That average is mostly dragged down by Victoria Coren Mitchell (2.42 points per task), Phil Wang (2.46 points per task) and David Baddiel (2.56 points per task).

DOES THIS MEAN ALL HIGHER EDUCATION IS POINTLESS?
Look, we just provide *Taskmaster* stats here. All we're saying is Ivo has an English degree from Oxford and he couldn't tell the difference between the word 'caravan' and the word 'shed'.

THE HISTORY OF THE WORLD AS TOLD BY TASKMASTER CONTESTANTS

Taskmaster contestants are frequently made to educate the public on their understanding of history. Here are their findings. Please do not use this as revision material for any actual history tests.

Some time before the year 1123: Pangea breaks up.

Prehistoric times: A dinosaur with the voice of Sophie Duker watches as her father, a dinosaur with the voice of Alex Horne, is exploded by a meteorite. It is very emotional.

Just after prehistoric times: Queen Nefertiti, as played by Judi Love, exists near some traffic cone pyramids. It is not very emotional.

Around zero: Jesus dies, according to Mae Martin.

1100: Birth of Owain ap Gwynedd, whom Greg Davies is NOT related to, according to Bridget Christie.

1122: Not the year 1123, according to Mae Martin.

1123: 'Rome has fallen. Christianity sweeps Europe. We're talking monotheism, baby! Some monks are bald.' – Professor Mae Martin

1124: Not the year 1123, according to Mae Martin.

1125: 'You can shout "medieval" at any point during this year. Life is hard, death frequent, tension constant. William the Conqueror might be dead and his son William Rufus might also be dead. France is a constant threat. The ancestors of Ivo Graham were born in a very narrow family tree. Oh no, I'm inbred.' – Professor Ivo Graham

13th century: Cats exist, according to Frankie Boyle, and are weird.

The Past (1200s): Cats exist, according to James Acaster, and it's good luck to put them in the walls of houses.

1417: 'The king is some sort of brutal English bastard who didn't know about atomic theory, central heating, the rapture and tobacco.' – Professor Frankie Boyle

1500: 'Water wasn't invented in this year, but it was used. Witches existed. It was a good year for farmers. Dogs, people and huts all existed.' – Professor Kiell Smith-Bynoe

1536: Henry VIII (who looks a lot like Jo Brand) cuts off the head of Anne Boleyn (who looks a lot like Alex Horne) and puts it on a platter outside the Taskmaster shed.

1558: A Tudor queen licks a lizard and starts to hallucinate several armless mannequins floating past her head. She then says, 'Bloody Nora I'm flying,' before jumping into the air.

1559: Kerry Godliman travels back in time to the Tudory Times to have a photo taken of herself in a fez.

1618: Several defenestrations take place in Prague, upsetting Dara Ó Briain 400 years later.

1642: 'A time of turmoil. A time of conflict. A time of weather. A time of women not having the kind of underwear we have today. Men might have been wearing the codpiece. Things that didn't exist for women yet: the pill, Ryvita and extra-large swans.' – Professor Jenny Eclair

Early 1800s: Enormous pigs are bred as part of the Agrarian Revolution (later popularised by Sally Phillips).

7 / NO STARS FOR NAUGHTY BOYS

The Past (assumed 1800s): According to John Robins, people sat on elephants' backs on big chairs (howdahs), and that was very cruel.

1912: Sue Perkins' great great great aunt Margaret survives the Titanic disaster, along with several priceless glass swans (later destroyed in the Taskmaster studio, 2023).

1943: Russia pushes the German forces back from Stalingrad armed with nothing but two traffic cones and an excitable Ardal O'Hanlon. The Russians celebrate wildly by singing 'It's a Long Way to Tipperary'.

1953: North and South Korea are divided (as told by Alex Horne through the medium of funk-disco break dance).

1957: Laika the dog is sent into space armed with nothing but a pot lid and a traffic cone. Much to Bridget Christie's sorrow, she does not make it back. Poor Laika. We did like her.

1989: The publication of Timmy Mallet's *Utterly Brilliant!* changes Jessica Knappett's life (because it gets her disqualified from a task, ultimately costing her the chance to win her series of *Taskmaster*).

1996: Dolly, a conical headless sheep, is cloned by Chris Ramsey, who immediately bursts into tears and asks if science has gone too far.

2004: The best thing from the 1990s according to Kerry Godliman (a complete DVD boxset of *Friends*) is released.

2015: *Taskmaster* is shown on television for the first time.

2019: Britain is attacked by a giant chicken with Johnny Vegas' voice.

The Distant Future: Everyone is blindfolded and hiding from robot vacuum cleaners, as prophesied by Lucy Beaumont.

The Year 3000: There is hail the size of houses and the sea is on fire, as prophesied by Charlotte Ritchie and Jamali Maddix.

FACTS ABOUT EGGS 3

🥚 Did you know that eggs do not float if you fill them with helium? Yes, obviously. But Mawaan Rizwan didn't know that. In Series 10, episode 1 he took the helium canister that was supposed to be used to create a little hot air balloon to float an egg down and decided to cut out the middle man by filling an egg with helium. Alex allowed Mawaan to make a little hole in his egg and daintily placed the nozzle inside the egg. With great confidence and focus, Mawaan turned the nozzle on the helium canister and the egg immediately exploded. 'OK. I've just wasted an egg.'

🥚 Even though it was only the first episode of the series, Greg understood the significance of what had just happened here. 'When people look back on this series, they will all in unison say, "That was the series where a grown man tried to fill an egg with helium."' Katherine Parkinson tried to stand up for Mawaan, saying that it was an inspired idea that could've worked (???), but under pressure from Greg ('You don't believe that, Katherine'), she wilted. Mawaan desperately looked for more validation from Katherine, but there was none. He was on his own in his little helium egg delusion.

SCHOOL TASKING
By Alex

My own children don't watch *Taskmaster*.

This is a frustrating situation for me, because I think they'd love *Taskmaster*. It seems to be a show that other families can sit down in front of and watch together, with various aspects appealing to various generations. With the advent of streaming, YouTube and such-like, it has become harder to find programmes that can unify age-groups, but, alas, my own household refuses to tune in.

The reason is that I'm in it quite a bit. And I take my clothes off quite a bit. And sometimes I sit on a cake after having removed my clothes. So I understand why my kids don't want to witness their father doing that sort of thing.

Nevertheless, I have been determined to get them involved one way or another, so as well as testing new task ideas on them at home, I signed up to running a *Taskmaster* day at their primary school, when our eldest was aged ten and in Year 6.

Despite the weirdness of having his dad, wearing a Marks and Spencer black suit, in his classroom, the day was a success. As soon as we'd all got over the awkwardness of me formally introducing myself, everyone relaxed and threw themselves into the jobs at hand.

The kids estimated the length of a ball of string by wrapping fellow pupils up, stretching it across the football field or making fairly abstract guesses. They created big circles by holding hands in groups or using their jumpers as home-made compasses. Without realising it they learned something about themselves, their imagination and their ambition, while having fun.

What I didn't realise was that other schools had also spotted the potential of using tasks to engage kids. Down in Sussex at a school called Sidlesham Primary, for instance, a teacher called James Blake-Lobb was holding far better organised *Taskmaster* events that quickly became the talk of his students. Like me, he loved the fact that it wasn't necessarily the sportiest or most numerically gifted kids that thrived, it was those that worked as a team, came up with outside-the-box ideas or who just tried really hard to have a laugh.

Meanwhile, a university professor called Ali Struthers had the idea that *Taskmaster* might help in her quest to widen participation in the law, by teaching kids from all backgrounds to think laterally and communally. She sent me a long message that included the following passages:

'I just wanted to let you know about a project that I'm currently developing at Warwick Law School, in collaboration with the Universities of Leicester and Edinburgh (we're working with ... James Blake-Lobb, who is helping us from the perspective of his *Taskmaster* teaching expertise!).

The project, School Tasking, has the ultimate aim of getting kids from schools in disadvantaged areas interested in coming to university to study law (though if successful, it could be rolled out to other subjects, such flexibility being the absolute beauty of *Taskmaster*) ...'

We all agreed this was a good idea and that James should be formally brought on board and soon we celebrated the twin births of School Tasking and Taskmaster Education. Here's Ali explaining the difference between the two projects:

7 / NO STARS FOR NAUGHTY BOYS

'School Tasking is an outreach project created at Warwick Law School and now running as a competition at universities across the UK and Ireland. It uses the format of *Taskmaster* to get Year 5s from schools in less advantaged areas enthusiastic about the idea of university study through fun, interactive and competitive tasks based on their learning during the project. It is free and only available to eligible primary schools.

'Taskmaster Education takes the joy and silliness of *Taskmaster* and uses it across various educational settings to encourage the development of key life skills with children and young people. Taskmaster Education runs Taskmaster Clubs, nationally and internationally, alongside live events for children, content in *AQUILA* magazine and charity initiatives, like our partnership with the children's mental health charity, Place2Be.'

Reading that, it does seem extraordinary how far a simple idea can reach and is a good lesson to me in the value of being open to suggestions and embracing enthusiastic people who want to get on board with a project. Also, mainly, nearly everyone likes fun.

AN ABSOLUTE CASSEROLE

DR LITTLE ALEX HORNE'S INAUGURATION SPEECH

Hello everyone,

I hope you're all having a lovely day. I'm having a very nice time and I'm extremely excited that my name is now Dr Little Alex Horne.

When I was told about today's event, I was given the following ... instructions by the university. I suppose you could call it a ... task:

Receive a degree from the University of Warwick.

When you do so, you must make a short speech in response.

You have no more than four-and-a-half minutes.

Your time starts now.

So here we go. I should explain that I make a show called *Taskmaster* on TV. I'm aware many of you might not know it, because it is quite a cult show, and you are important people with important things to do. But just to explain it

7 / NO STARS FOR NAUGHTY BOYS

briefly, on the show five comedians compete against each other doing ridiculous tasks that I set. That's it. And the tasks are meant to be amusing or at least intriguing.

If we had a task like 'Give a short speech in response,' we'd probably add another layer or two. Something like, 'Your short speech must be inspiring, surprising, amusing, powerful, original and truly moving – and short – and also you may not use the letter F at all. And you must wink at least six times during your speech. So rom now on, that's what I'm going to try to do (WINK).

Good luck, everyone. Twenty twenty-our is a big year or me. Because twenty twenty-our is a leap year. So it's one day bigger than a normal year. But it's also big because in June my wie and I are going to a dinner to mark twenty-ive years a-ter we both started university. We're also going to be celebrating our twentieth wedding anniversary at the end o this year. It's de-initely a big year.

So starting this big year with this big occasion is both exciting and humbling. When I inished my own university, I did not have a plan. I had not been to career airs and I had not done any sort o apprenticeship. I'd done zero networking and I didn't know what I wanted to do or a living.

What I had done was made a lot o riends – good pals – including my wie, and I'd had a lot o un. You know – UN. Excitement! Entertainment! Amusement! (WINK) I'd played sport, written on the university newspaper and started doing stand-up comedy. Looking back, I realise now that I have essentially carried on doing those things or a quarter o a century, but without lectures or essays getting in the way. It really has been a UN twenty-IVE years.

So, how have I managed to end up on TV and, more importantly, on this stage getting a doctorate? Well, I think it's down to our things. The irst, is good ortune. I've been lukey again and again in my career. Anyone who can make a living as a comedian has to rely on various elicitous elements (WINK).

But some o that luck is made by persistence. I have always worked hard, even i that work is really just mucking about. I've also always had a weird, almost stubborn aith — or belie — that things will be OK. Again, to put all your eggs in the comedy basket, you have to be optimistic.

But the biggest reason why I'm here today is nothing to do with me, it's to do with other people. I've always had a knack of be-riending other more talented people than me. And I think that's a very handy knack to have.

This honorary degree, I was told, is 'speciically a Doctor o Letters in recognition o the support and commitment you have made through our School Tasking outreach programme with primary schools with the School o Law, which is now being rolled out as a national competition.'

You've already been told some details about what School Tasking is, but here's what it means to me. School Tasking is a project that could not have been thought up by me — or by AI. It's the result o years o playing and working hard, o both academic rigour and complete nonsense; it's the privilege o the television world and the generosity

7 / NO STARS FOR NAUGHTY BOYS

o education combining to make something odd, UN and intriguing or children. It's something I'm immensely proud o and always surprised by (WINK).

So I'm being given this honorary doctorate (WINK), because I've supported a programme that other people have been ar more responsible or (and by other people I mainly mean Dr Ali Struthers). And she may say that the programme I make was what launched the programme she makes, but my programme is made by about 100 other people, so I'm just one per cent o that — and I had the chance to make that programme thanks to another one hundred people who helped me get to that position, so that's one per cent o one per cent which means I've only actually earned a tiny percentage o this doctorate mysel.

And yet, I am here, very happily accepting it, partly because it's a wonder-ul thing, but also because I do so on behal o Dr Struthers and her team and everyone who works on *Taskmaster* and the children who have embraced the nonsense. And I want to dedicate it to anyone who doesn't really know what they're going to do in in their lives.

I think it's absolutely OK not to know what you want to do. It's OK not to have a plan. With a bit o luck, hard work, optimism and the support o those around you, everything will be OK.

So thank you very much or this. And congratulations to everyone else who has worked so hard to get their actual degrees today at this antastic, abulous and very ashionable occasion (WINK). Airwell.

TASKMASTER HALL OF GLORY
Most Episode Wins

NAME: Richard Herring

NUMBER OF EPISODE WINS: 5

SERIES: 10

SERIES POINTS: 162 (3.18 points per task)

POSITION IN SERIES: First, thanks to a last-minute pasta marshmallow collapse from Daisy May Cooper

FUN FACT: Richard scored fewer points in his series than any of the other champions in Champion of Champions 2, but despite this he went on to win.

GREATEST ACHIEVEMENT: Gorging on watermelon with Daisy May Cooper in a disturbing animalistic feast.

LOWEST MOMENT: Trying to make a massive beermat house on the table and ring the doorbell at the same time, he ended up giving himself a massive beermat papercut and smearing blood over the doorbell.

RELEVANT QUOTE: 'Failure! Failure! Failure!'

7 / NO STARS FOR NAUGHTY BOYS

Edinburgh Task 6: How Did It Go?

In early 2010, Twitter was just getting established when Mark Watson tweeted to his then impressive 18,000 followers that I was magnificent. Over on more mainstream media, James Dowdeswell broadcast the same message on BRMB Birmingham radio to a listenership of over a million, while Mark Olver did so in Bristol and Rosie Long used BBC 6 Music.

Henning Wehn took out an advert on Chortle (the foremost comedy website in the country) at great expense, while someone else (still a mystery) hacked into my email account and added it as my regular signature at the bottom of all future emails.

The winner was Stuart Goldsmith who persuaded the Loose Women to describe me as such, live on air, in part two of the show on Tuesday 2 March 2010, something that resulted in a telling off for Stu from the producer and exactly zero people noticing.

All these attempts demonstrated that not only do comics tend to have contacts in the media and with the general public, they are also not afraid to use and abuse those contacts in order to win an extra, largely meaningless, point. In short, comedians enjoy creating mischief with people.*

> *See also Joe Lycett's *Where's Wally?* tribute (series 4, episode 4) where he attempted to camouflage himself by crouching beside ten members of the public and Al Murray, all wearing matching stripy jumpers, and Rhod Gilbert's attempt to emulate a Space Invaders computer game (series 7, episode 10) by throwing tennis balls at a large crowd of people.

EDINBURGH TASK 7
1 March 2010

Good afternoon one and all.

First, I very much appreciate your inventive and successful spreading of my magnificence. Some truly excellent work. You will receive the most up-to-date league table within a week or two. Meanwhile it's time for this month's task:

THE DRINKING RACE

Yes, it's the inevitable competition to see who can down a pint quickest.

The deal is this: film yourself drinking a pint (of any liquid you like) as quickly as possible then send me the clip (it can be on a mobile phone, home-video-camera, cinefilm, whatever you can lay your hands on).

I'll then stick them all together somehow, so we can have a great big drinking race and see who gets this month's points. Good good.

One other thing — the first five people to send me their entries will be rewarded with one of the signed celebrity photos I have in my collection (these are genuine autographed snaps, signed by the actual people, and include the likes of Frank Bruno (the boxer) and Tony Benn (not the boxer — that's Nigel).

7 / NO STARS FOR NAUGHTY BOYS

And one further thing, a certain Mr Goldsmith was rather outraged that I only gave you a month to complete the last magnificent challenge. I quote: 'Hang on a minute, what's all this "week left" bullshit? There was nothing on the brief to suggest this was a timed mission!'

I must admit I thought it was understood that unless otherwise stated, each of these challenges should be completed within the calendar month. I apologise if that wasn't clear and was 'bullshit'.

So, if you do need a bit more time to tell people I'm magnificent you can, on this occasion, have until the end of March to do so (although those of you who got their entries in on time will be heavily favoured in the scoring).

That is all. Please try not to accuse me of 'bullshit' too often.

Yours,

The Taskmaster

BMX-ING!

TASKMASTER AND SPORT

We all love sport. Except the Taskmaster, who hates it. So actually, maybe we should all hate sport? In seventeen series there have been some amazing sporting achievements and there was also the time Lolly tried to luge down a concrete driveway. Pop on a Plymouth Argyle shirt from the 1990s and cheer like you're watching Alex Horne trying to chip a ball over a giant wagon wheel, because this is MULTI-SPORT!

LITTLE ALEX'S HORSE

It was almost exactly five years after Andy and I staged a game of cricket on horseback at Shardeloes Farm Equestrian Centre that we returned, with Frank Skinner, Josh Widdicombe, Roisin Conaty, Romesh Ranganathan and Tim Key, to tackle one of the most show's memorable tasks: Paint the best picture of a horse whilst riding a horse.

To celebrate the influence these creatures have had on the little life of Alex Horne, here are some equine facts:

- Horses can sleep standing up or lying down
- Horses can neither burp nor vomit
- Horses cannot breathe through their mouths
- Horses have excellent memories, can hear well and are good at swimming
- Horses have an almost 360-degree field of vision, but have two blind spots – one directly in front and one directly behind
- A herd of horses will never all lie down at the same time
- A horse produces ten gallons of saliva every day
- A horse's heart is the same size as a basketball
- Fifty million years ago, horses were the same size as dogs
- The longest horse tail measured twelve foot six inches
- A horse's teeth take up more space in its head than its brain
- Horses have bigger eyes than any other land mammal, including elephants
- In New York it is illegal to open or close an umbrella in the presence of a horse.

SPORTING ACHIEVEMENTS

Some contestants are not just good at comedy – they're also, upsettingly, surprisingly good at sport. Here is a list of some of the greatest sporting achievements in *Taskmaster* history.

Hugh Dennis is a glorious bag baller

TASK: Score the best goal with this plastic bag

EPISODE: Series 4, episode 6 ('Spatchcock It')

SPORTSPERSON: Hugh Dennis

SPORT: Bagball

WHAT HAPPENED: In a task where contestants had to score a goal with the plastic bag in as few kicks as possible, Hugh tucked the bag ball into his sock with his other foot. He sprinted down the pitch to the goal, before executing a perfect forward roll over the goal line to the whooping and cheering fans (who, according to Greg, had only been given to Hugh because the show felt sorry for him).

SPEED: 1 minute, 51 seconds (and no penalties for kicking it)

RELEVANT QUOTE: 'I've never seen a reaction in the studio like that in my life, Hugh. Someone got so excited they shouted out "Awooga!"' – Greg Davies congratulating Hugh

Noel Fielding smashes a mini-cheese

TASK: Strike one of these objects the furthest distance with one of the other objects, in three attempts

EPISODE: Series 4, episode 8 ('Tony Three Pies')

SPORTSPERSON: Noel Fielding

SPORT: Golf+

WHAT HAPPENED: Armed with a pool cue and a mini-cheese in a red wax coating, Fielding snapped the pool cue in half to aid his swing before striking the cheese in a perfect drive, like prime Rory McIlroy.

DISTANCE: 29.6 metres

RELEVANT QUOTE: 'The more I see you, you're just a lad. All these clothes are just for telly, at the weekend, when you're out, they call you "Tony Three Pies".' – Greg Davies, rumbling Noel's sporty persona

Sally Phillips tosses the jelly

TASK: Eat one item; balance one item on the pole; throw an item in the bucket from behind the rope

EPISODE: Series 5, episode 3 ('Phoenix')

SPORTSPERSON: Sally Phillips

SPORT: Jelly toss

WHAT HAPPENED: With a determined concentration, Phillips moved the table to balance the Weetabix and ate the Twiglet, before readying herself for the jelly shot. In one smooth motion and with devastating accuracy she tossed the jelly into the bucket. Back in the studio the audience were on their feet and Greg embraced the clear winner. It's footage that will be used to train the next generation of jelly tossers.

SPEED: 2 minutes, 1 second

RELEVANT QUOTE: 'I've got three children and that's pretty much how we feed them.' – Alex Horne

Russell Howard bowls a wicket

TASK: Knock the bails off the stumps. You have a maximum of one over (six throws)

EPISODE: Series 6, episode 7 ('Roadkill Doused in Syrup')

SPORTSPERSON: Russell Howard

SPORT: Cricket

WHAT HAPPENED: Discarding all the other balls available to him, Russell picked up the cricket ball and bowled a perfect yorker.

SPEED: 21 seconds

RELEVANT QUOTE: 'It's a lot easier when there's no batsman.' – Russell Howard

Lou Sanders makes pan hoop history

TASK: Choose a hoop to throw a frying pan into, then choose a distance to throw from. Longest distance from a successful throw wins

EPISODE: Series 8, episode 4 (The Barrel Dad')

SPORTSPERSON: Lou Sanders

SPORT: Pan hoop

WHAT HAPPENED: Going into the final throw, it looked as if Paul Sinha's conservative tactic had paid off; he had placed a hoop very close and was the only contestant to land a pan. Then up stepped Lou Sanders, who had placed her hoop right at the end of the Knappett. 'Imagine if it does go in,' Greg mumbled to himself. With one throw to go, Lou tossed the pan … straight into the hoop, skidding it slightly, but with just enough backspin to ensure it stayed on the stage. The crowd went crazy and I swear Greg choked back a tear.

RELEVANT QUOTE: 'That was a pretty sport-defining moment for pan hoop.' – Greg Davies

Alan Davies is a great goalkeeper

TASK: Prevent Alex from scoring a goal. Slowest goal scored by Alex wins

EPISODE: Series 12, episode 5 ('Croissants is Croissants')

SPORTSPERSON: Alan Davies

SPORT: Football

WHAT HAPPENED: Alan Davies' tactic was to put the goal face down, so that the only scorable part was facing the caravan, and then move several large items to block it (Linda the Cow, the piano, the big wagon wheel). After a few attempts, Alex started to move items out/put the goal on blocks to create gaps to score, at which point Alan moved into the goal, crouching down, trying to keep the ball out like a crab David Seaman. For a while this tactic worked, a few remarkable saves from Davies kept the score level (including one Neuer-esque parry with his foot), until eventually one crept in at Davies' far post. The defence was breached, but it was a heroic effort by the veteran Arsenal man.

TIME: 9 minutes, 47 minutes

RELEVANT QUOTE: 'We were basically wrestling by the end.' – Alex Horne

Chris Ramsey enters the Sausage Arena

TASK: Use the cement mixer for something other than mixing cement

EPISODE: Series 13, episode 6 ('The 75th Question')

SPORTSPERSON: Chris Ramsey

SPORT: Sausage mixer

WHAT HAPPENED: Chris Ramsey invented a new potential Olympic sport by strapping two sausages with different coloured ribbons to a cement mixer; first one to successfully eat their sausage would win. What he hadn't checked was the speed of the cement mixer. It was unfathomably fast, to the point that both Chris and Alex looked genuinely terrified that they would be killed by a speeding sausage. Mouths, noses, faces were all struck by the orbiting pork pole, until eventually the mixer stopped, allowing Chris the chance to chew his way to victory.

POINTS FOR SPORT INVENTION: 5

RELEVANT QUOTE: 'Rarely have I seen a sausage go from still to accelerating that fast.' – Chris Ramsey

Joanne McNally sets a European record

TASK: Hoopla Gary

EPISODE: Series 17, episode 1 ('Grappling With My Life')

SPORTSPERSON: Joanne McNally

SPORT: Gorilla ring toss

WHAT HAPPENED: In a task where Sophie Willan nearly drowned trying to hop over a river, Joanne McNally showed everyone how it was done. She spotted Gary the Gorilla coming down the waterway in a little canoe, steadied herself and chucked the ring over him with a minimum of fuss. Steve Pemberton and John Robins also did well, but at this level margins matter and it was the young Irish athlete who won out.

SPEED: 48 seconds (a new European record, apparently)

RELEVANT QUOTE: 'All three of you at the end of the day … it's not exciting, but you did quite well.' – Greg Davies, begrudgingly

GREG HATES FOOTBALL

You don't need to be a stats nerd to know that if you want to win at *Taskmaster*, it might be a good idea to appeal to Greg's tastes. Related fact: Greg HATES football and will punish any mention of it.

1 SERIES 1, EPISODE 1: Josh Widdicome brought in a football signed by the Plymouth Argyle squad that lost the Division Two 1994 play-off finals (but the signatures had rubbed off).
POINTS AWARDED BY GREG: 1

2 SERIES 1, EPISODE 2: Romesh Ranganathan brought in a cap thrown from the Arsenal tour bus after winning the 2001/02 Double, although Josh Widdicombe pointed out it could have been thrown from the other side of the bus.
RELEVANT QUOTE: 'I can't bear football. When I'm king it'll be banned.' – Greg Davies
POINTS AWARDED BY GREG: 1

3 SERIES 1, EPISODE 6: Josh Widdicombe brought in a finished 2014 World Cup sticker album that took him three months to complete, spending weeks swapping stickers with other grown men.
RELEVANT QUOTE: 'But, the last time I was interested in a football album was in 1982 and that's not 'cause I like football, it was to impress a boy called Philip.' – Greg Davies
POINTS AWARDED BY GREG: 1

4 SERIES 3, EPISODE 3: As a gift for the Taskmaster, Dave Gorman bought Greg a programme for Wem Town FC's biggest ever game, as he learned on Facebook that Greg supports Wem Town FC.

RELEVANT QUOTE: 'I didn't know [Wem Town FC] existed, genuinely. Genuinely.' – Greg Davies

POINTS AWARDED BY GREG: 5, but that was more because of the other Wem-themed gifts that Dave got for Greg and Greg's desire to give Shropshire a shout-out on TV

5 SERIES 3, EPISODE 4: Rob Beckett brought in another (nearly) completed World Cup sticker album.

RELEVANT QUOTE: 'I despise football. I got a Panini sticker just to try to fit in.' – Greg Davies

POINTS AWARDED BY GREG: 2

6 SERIES 3, EPISODE 5: Paul Chowdhry did keepie-uppies for the 'Do something that looks brilliant sped up or slowed down' task.

RELEVANT QUOTE: 'You did boast a lot about your football skills before. It was the ninth take before you did it, but ...' – Alex Horne

POINTS AWARDED BY GREG: Despite saying that it was 'genuinely good', he only gave it 3 points

7 SERIES 4, EPISODE 2: Hugh Dennis brought in his loser's medal for the National Public School six-a-side football tournament from when he was eighteen, for 'Most boastful thing'.

RELEVANT QUOTE: 'Did you understand what we wanted?' – Greg Davies

POINTS AWARDED BY GREG: 1

8 / BMX-ING!

8 SERIES 5, EPISODE 7: Bob Mortimer brought in yet another completed 2014 World Cup sticker album for the most surprisingly expensive item. Greg guessed it would cost £20; the show had it valued at £10.

POINTS AWARDED BY GREG: 3

9 SERIES 6, EPISODE 4: Russell Howard played football for having the most fun (while Alice Levine had a bath).

RELEVANT QUOTE: 'I like watching Russell Howard keep a football up in the air.' – Greg Davies in a rare moment of football admiration

POINTS AWARDED BY GREG: 2

10 SERIES 6, EPISODE 8: Russell Howard brought in shoes owned by Liverpool footballer Philippe Coutinho for 'Most interesting footwear'.

RELEVANT QUOTE: 'I find verrucas slightly less interesting than football.' – Greg Davies

POINTS AWARDED BY GREG: 2

11 SERIES 6, EPISODE 8: Russell Howard put several genuinely surprising things inside a chocolate egg, including a trip for two to watch Liverpool FC (which Alex did take advantage of, with his son and Russell).

POINTS AWARDED BY GREG: 3

12 **SERIES 12, EPISODE 6:** Victoria Coren Mitchell brought in part of a season ticket for Manchester United, intended for one of the most famous Arsenal fans in the world, Alan Davies.

POINTS AWARDED BY GREG: 1, but he did appreciate how fabulous it was as an awful gift

RELEVANT QUOTE: 'It's the most passive-aggressive, calculated personal attack that I've ever experienced.' – Alan Davies

13 **SERIES 14, EPISODE 2:** Dara Ó Briain brought in a bit of his leg that snapped off during a football game.

POINTS AWARDED BY GREG: 5, but that wasn't really to do with the football and more to do with the bit of leg

RELEVANT QUOTE: 'It's made my balls go up inside me.' – Greg Davies, on Dara's description of the injury

THE NEED FOR SPEED

Usain Bolt. Mo Farah. Liza Tarbuck. All people dedicated to getting stuff done QUICKLY. Although in Liza's case it was usually because there was a taxi waiting and she wanted to get home quicker. Here are some of the fastest attempts in the show's history.

5th place

TASK: Pop the balloons as quickly as possible

EPISODE: Series 3, episode 2 ('The Dong and the Gong')

CONTESTANT: Rob Beckett

TIME ACHIEVED: 31.6 seconds

WHAT HAPPENED: While the feral Sara Pascoe and Dave Gorman used their teeth to pop balloons, Rob Beckett took a further evolutionary leap and discovered tools. Armed with two corkscrews, he swiped at the balloons 'like a sort of angry cat' and completed the task in just over 30 seconds. There are times when this show transcends light entertainment and instead becomes like watching someone's rage therapy session.

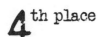

4th place

TASK: Knock the bails off the stumps

EPISODE: Series 6, episode 7 ('Roadkill Doused in Syrup')

CONTESTANT: Russell Howard

TIME ACHIEVED: 21 seconds

WHAT HAPPENED: While Tim Vine used cunning to knock the bails off the stumps by carefully winding a piece of string around the stump and pulling (a tactic they don't approve of in the County Championship), and Liza Tarbuck resorted to barrelling it over with an oil drum (ditto), it was the sportsman Russell Howard who stepped up and bowled a perfect ball first time. 'Call me when I'm needed,' he yelled out as he sauntered off after just 21 seconds.

3rd place

TASK: Light the candle in the caravan

EPISODE: Series 5, episode 6 ('Spoony Neeson')

CONTESTANT: Aisling Bea

TIME ACHIEVED: 9 seconds (failed)

WHAT HAPPENED: This task was all about carefully keeping the flame lit as one edged through the house. While other contestants took their time and thought about the task – Sally Phillips found a bell jar, Mark Watson mostly just paced back and forth muttering 'fiddly' until the flame went out – Aisling Bea tried a novel approach: run as fast as possible. She opened the door of the lab, caused a backdraft and instantly extinguished the candle. Look, they can't all be winners, can they?

2nd place

TASK: Knock over the ducks

8 / BMX-ING!

EPISODE: Series 4, episode 1 ('A Fat Bald White Man')
CONTESTANT: Hugh Dennis
TIME ACHIEVED: 8.09 seconds
WHAT HAPPENED: Because Hugh Dennis had a habit of bringing in cloud newsletters for his prize tasks, it's easy to forget that he was actually quite good at *Taskmaster*. In fact he was the best in his series at objectively judged tasks, and this was a great example. He lined his ducks in a row with some well-placed rope, gave it a tug and took them all down in a time faster than Usain Bolt (although, as Hugh pointed out, this isn't exactly the event that Usain is known for).

1st place

TASK: Drink all this drink with your mouth open
EPISODE: Series 12, episode 10 ('Caring Uncle Minpict')
CONTESTANT: Desiree Burch
TIME ACHIEVED: 7 seconds
WHAT HAPPENED: Every other contestant struggled with this task – Victoria Coren Mitchell doubted that completing this one was even possible (although, to be fair, she said that during most of her tasks) – but Desiree Burch blew everyone away by drinking a glass of water with her mouth wide open in just seven seconds. 'I don't mind telling you, it's left me a little unsettled,' Greg murmured, but for Desiree it was just a normal day in the office. This is the woman who had, in a previous task, eaten some sand for no reason whatsoever. She was always going to win this one.

TASKMASTER HALL OF GLORY

Best Contestant in the Lab

NAME: Liza Tarbuck

NUMBER OF POINTS SCORED IN THE LAB: 27 from six tasks (4.50 points per task)

SERIES POINTS: 181 (3.23 points per task)

POSITION IN SERIES: First

BEST MOMENT IN THE LAB: During the team task, where Liza (along with Tim Vine and Asim Chaudhry) had to work out the link between several clues and then do it one hundred times. Liza worked out they had to hop, told Tim and Asim they had to hop, was ignored for five minutes and then decided to hop one hundred times all on her own. As Greg said, there has never been a clearer metaphor for the plight of women through the ages.

FUN FACT: If there were no lab tasks in series 6, Liza would have finished the series level with Tim Vine at the top …

RELEVANT QUOTE: 'Greg's going to bloody demolish me for that!' – Tim Vine after the task, according to Liza Tarbuck

> **Edinburgh Task 7: How Did It Go?**
>
> There were some impressively quick drinking times which foreshadowed several tasks from the TV show (like the very first watermelon gobbling by Tim Key and Romesh Ranganathan). But, like Roisin's attempt in that inaugural episode, the most intriguing were by those who got it slightly wrong; Lloyd Langford got muddled and smashed a pint glass on his head, Joe Wilkinson drank rainwater and Mike Wozniak did it with milk (in 9.4 seconds).

EDINBURGH TASK 8
1 April 2010

Dear all,

Here is this month's task. It won't take you long. But you do have to follow these instructions carefully:

A LOVELY LOVE SONG

You're each going to write two lines of a song. One by one. A bit like consequences (a game that my Aunt Polly likes). It'll work like this:

AN ABSOLUTE CASSEROLE

I write the first line and send it to the first person on the alphabetical list below. They write their reply to me with a line that follows my line, then send another single line to the person below them on the alphabetical list.

Every time I should be cc'ed in so I can check it's working.

It will work.

And every other line must begin: LOVE IS LIKE A...

For example, I might start with:

LOVE IS LIKE A BUTTERFLY

Mr Atkinson might then reply with:

IT MAKES YOU STOP AND SMILE AND SIGH.

Then send something like the following to Mr Basden:

LOVE IS LIKE A WOODEN DESK

Mr Basden would then reply with a line saying why love is like a wooden desk, before sending another 'LOVE IS LIKE A...' to Mr Christmas.

And so on. Lines don't have to rhyme. Or scan. Or be just one line. They should be lovely. Best lines win the points.

That's it. We should have the song licked in a month. I'll then put it to music and release it or something.

So, in short, you don't have to do anything till you're sent a LOVE IS LIKE A... line. Then you reply with your next line. And send the beginning of the next couplet to the person below you on the list (cc'ing me in). Easy.

Here's the list: REDACTED

In other news — not all the pint-downings are in yet — yes, you can have short extensions. But please send me a clip (from your phone or whatever) of you drinking a pint of something asap. If you want to do it in front of me so I can film it, no problem. We can do that while playing some sort of sport.

Finally, the results of this year's challenge will be revealed in the Queen Dome just after midnight on Friday 27 August (i.e. very early in the morning on Saturday 28 August). If you think you might be able to be there, please let me know. You should be there. I will provide you with beer and comps. And possibly the prize. If you win.

Good luck.

Good bye.

Good times?

The Taskmaster

9

ROADKILL DOUSED IN SYRUP

TASKMASTER AND FOOD

In many ways, *Taskmaster* is exactly like *Masterchef*. A bunch of people do things to please a big angry man who shouts at them. Also, sometimes there's food involved. Get ready to take a culinary tour through *Taskmaster* – the drinks, the meals and the entire gastronomical experience. (NB: *Taskmaster* does not take responsibility for any food poisoning that may result in attempting to recreate any of the following.)

A LIST OF SOME OF THE FINEST COCKTAILS FEATURED ON TASKMASTER

Daisy May Cooper's 'F*** Sake'

- Tiny serving of warm vodka
- Tiny lime juice
- Unopened umbrella

Johnny Vegas' 'Cloudy Mule'

- Coke
- Champagne served in his spit
- Lemon
- Lime
- Sparklers

Katherine Parkinson's 'Milk'

- Milk

Richard Herring's 'The Doesn't Matterhorne'

- Vodka
- Rhubarb drink
- Olives

9 / ROADKILL DOUSED IN SYRUP

Mawaan Rizwan's 'Bin Juice'

- Wine
- Milk
- Egg
- Bin juice
- Strands of hair
- Bits of mud
- Garnished with orange slices, an unopened umbrella and a bottle cap
- Bonus catchphrase: 'Gettin' trashed!'

GIVE ME SOME STATS:
Is it useful to be a vegan?

Hypothesis
Being a vegan helps you to win at *Taskmaster*.

WHERE DOES THIS COME FROM?
James from New Jersey, a listener of *Taskmaster: the People's Podcast*, which was then hosted by *Taskmaster* champion and vegan, Lou Sanders.

DETAILED METHODOLOGY TO OBTAIN DATA
Jack, as our resident *Taskmaster* stats guy, Googled 'Is [*Taskmaster* contestant] a vegan?' for all 85 *Taskmaster* contestants. When this didn't work, he consumed a lot of tangential media: specific episodes of the *Off Menu* podcast, a few hours of *Saturday Kitchen* and an episode of *Drifters* where Jessica Knappett's character eats a meat kebab.

SO, IS THIS INFORMATION AT ALL ACCURATE?
Look, do you want the stats or not?

WHAT DO THE STATS SAY?
We found 13 confirmed veggie or vegan contestants, including champions Josh Widdicombe, Kerry Godliman, Lou Sanders, Morgana Robinson and highest points scorer ever, John Robins. Vegans and veggies have a points per task average of 3.08. That

9 / ROADKILL DOUSED IN SYRUP

compares very favourably to the average of the meat and fish eating contestants, which was 2.96 points per task.

So, while it is admittedly a very small sample size, it seems that yes, veganism is the way to go to win *Taskmaster*. Although it does limit your ability to make surprisingly pleasant fish sausages.

TERRIBLE THINGS ALEX HAS EATEN

Alex loves to suffer for his art. By which we mean, having disgusting bits of food thrust into his face at the bidding of some of Britain's best-loved comedians. Here is a list of everything awful he's put in his mouth in the name of the show.

- Dog food tortellini, courtesy of Tim Key (series 1, episode 6)
- Hot toothpaste pie, forced upon him by Roisin Conaty (series 1, episode 2)
- Tea that Ed Gamble spat milk into (series 9, episode 10)
- Doughnut chewed by Lucy Beaumont (series 16, episode 10)
- Bread, egg, raw pepper, raw onion, mushroom, chocolate egg and Maltesers as part of Charlotte Ritchie's babushka meal (series 11, episode 7)
- Absinthe on toast, which Sally Phillips claimed to be Marmite (series 5, episode 4)
- A sausage made of skin, apple cider vinegar, 'ugly' raisins, spinach, artisanal seeds, grains and eggs (three) from Sam Campbell (series 16, episode 4).

FACTS ABOUT EGGS 4

🥚 Did you know that celebrated producer and bestselling author Richard Osman broke the record for fastest completion of a task by eating a raw egg in around five seconds? 'It wasn't my favourite thing I've ever done, but I had a nice cup of tea with me.' Once again, we must remind you not to eat raw eggs, despite the actions of your favourite murder mystery writer.

🥚 Who knew that wrapping up an egg in paper does not stop it from breaking when dropped on the ground? Frank Skinner found this out in the most devastating fashion in Series 1, when he tried to win the 'Get this egg the highest' task by covering his egg in pink craft paper and chucking it into the air. After he missed the catch (falling over in the process), he picked up the egg, unwrapped it, and let out a little sigh. 'Didn't work out. I ... I was so confident. I couldn't see anything going wrong.' Frank walked away with not just a broken egg, but a broken heart.

EVERY TIME BAKED BEANS HAVE APPEARED IN TASKMASTER UK

Series 1, episode 4: Josh had to count out how many beans in a tin of baked beans – he discovered there were 406, and that he was the most gullible of all the series 1 contestants.
FUN FACT: This task was referenced in the rolling text in the 'Most brilliant socially distanced sports' task in series 12. On the vidiprinter, the 'cricket score' 'JW Beans 406 not out' comes up. JW refers to Josh Widdicombe, while 406 refers to the number of beans.

Series 5, episode 8: Alex got Sally Phillips a tin of baked beans, but mispronounced it as 'tuna baked beans' (in order to make another one of his fish puns, in a task that only he knew he was competing in).

Series 5, episode 8: Rosalind tells Nish Kumar and Mark Watson that her favourite food is beans on toast. In their song, they tell her they want to 'serve her beans on toast, but it's a fantasy, it's nothing but a boast.'

Series 6, episode 1: The contestants had to sort objects under the table in order of size, using their feet, and one of the items in Russell Howard's collection was a tin of baked beans.

Series 7, episode 1: The contestants had to work out the circumference of the caravan in baked beans, in just three minutes. Greg stated that only a mad person would take a bean and move it up and down the caravan, and that is what all five of them immediately did.

AN ABSOLUTE CASSEROLE

FUN FACT: At one point in his terrible calculations, Phil Wang estimated there were 100 beans in a can. If he'd watched Josh Widdicombe's series, he'd have known he was out by a factor of four.

RELEVANT QUOTE: 'I know it's early days, but are we the stupidest so far?' – James Acaster, mid-bean breakdown

Series 8, episode 5: In a task to make the most horrific realistic injury, Iain Stirling made it look as if his leg bone had snapped in an accident with a tin of baked beans.

Series 14, episode 3: Dara Ó Briain brought in a segmented frying pan as a prize for 'The thing you most want on a Sunday morning', because it could specifically handle baked beans in one section, eggs in another. Greg was insulted at the suggestion that he didn't already own one.

TASKMASTERCHEF: THE BIG BOOK OF TASKMASTER RECIPES

Have you ever watched an episode of *Taskmaster* and thought 'Wow, that plate of barely cooked food that comedian has just served to Alex Horne for a task looks delicious! If only I could try it!' No? Really? OK, suit yourself. Anyway, here are some of the recipes of the most delicious/least hazardous to health meals on the show.

Tim Key's Citrus Faeces

TASK: Make the best meal for the Taskmaster using ingredients beginning with every letter of the alphabet (series 1, episode 6) You have a total of two hours.

Ingredients:

All bran	*Juice from a cow [milk]*	*Super chillies*
Back (bacon)	*Kettle Chips*	*Tequila*
Cheese spread	*Loyd Grossman sauce*	*Um Bongo*
Dog food	*Marg*	*V [unknown]*
Eggs	*Nutella/nachos?*	*Water sparkling*
Flour	*Onions*	*X-large grape*
Grapefruit	*Pheasant*	*Yop*
Hog	*Quince*	*Zebra*
Ink [?]	*Rabbit/red wine*	

Method:
1. Chop onions.
2. Place pheasant in a baking tray in preheated oven.

AN ABSOLUTE CASSEROLE

3. Prepare and pan fry zebra.
4. Pour a generous amount of red wine into a pot of meat and miscellaneous food items.
5. Roll out your pastry dough on a floured surface.
6. Place pastry in a dish and bake.
7. Drink fizzy water.
8. Start the pasta dough by adding Kettle Chips to a blender.
9. Mix the dough whilst shouting 'Oh god'.
10. Roll the dough out on a chopping board and evenly distribute spoonfuls of dog food across the dough.
11. Boil the ravioli.
12. Drop pheasant.
13. Carefully salvage pheasant by grabbing it with a tea towel and dropping it into a bowl.
14. Add Um Bongo, fizzy ice cubes, Yop and tequila to a mug.
15. Serve up with grapefruit.

Dave Gorman's Skull and Crossbones Surprise

TASK: Create the best flag meal (series 3, episode 3)
You have 10 minutes to choose your flag and plan your meal, then 30 minutes to prepare it. Best flag meal wins.

Ingredients:

Squid ink   *The finest champagne*   *Risotto rice*
Cauliflower   *Black-eyed beans*
Quails' eggs   *White rice noodles*

9 / ROADKILL DOUSED IN SYRUP

Method:
1. Chop cauliflower.
2. Pan fry cauliflower.
3. Drink champagne.
4. Boil rice.
5. Strain and mix squid ink while in colander.
6. Made a bed of the rice and add cauliflower for the head and bones.
7. Drink champagne.
8. Add rice noodles to form the cross.
9. Quails' eggs to be added as eyes.
10. Place 11 black-eyed beans to create the teeth.
11. Serve your Skull and Crossbones Surprise.

Mel Giedroyc's Chocolate Club Sandwich

TASK: Make the most exotic sandwich (series 4, episode 8)

You have ten minutes to plan your exotic sandwich, then ten minutes to construct it.

Ingredients:

Turkish delight	*M&Ms*	*Chocolate eggs*
Crunchie bars	*Chocolate spread*	*Marshmallows*
KitKat	*Maltesers*	*Sliced white bread*
Double Deckers	*Twix*	
Chocolate Oranges	*Snickers*	

Method:
1. Spread the chocolate spread onto an end piece of sliced white bread.
2. Add a good layer of Chocolate Orange segments.

3. Add another chocolate spread-covered slice of white bread.
4. Place Double Deckers atop of this layer.
5. Add another chocolate spread-covered slice of white bread.
6. Next, a layer of Crunchies.
7. More bread and then another layer of chocolate bars.
8. More bread and then a few handfuls of M&Ms.
9. More bread and a handful of Maltesers for the next layer.
10. For the final layer add chocolate spread and marshmallows to the bread.
11. Use a blow torch to bronze up the marshmallows.
12. You must now eat your exotic sandwich.

Bob Mortimer's Residue Around the Hoof Marmite

TASK: Make Marmite (series 5, episode 4)
You have ten minutes to select your ingredients and then ten minutes to make your Marmite. The best Marmite wins.

Ingredients:

Sugar substitute syrup   *Black food colouring*
Brown sauce   *Dark treacle*
Beef stock cubes   *Bovril*

Method:
1. Eat a bit of stock cube.
2. Mix the ingredients.
3. Pour into jar.

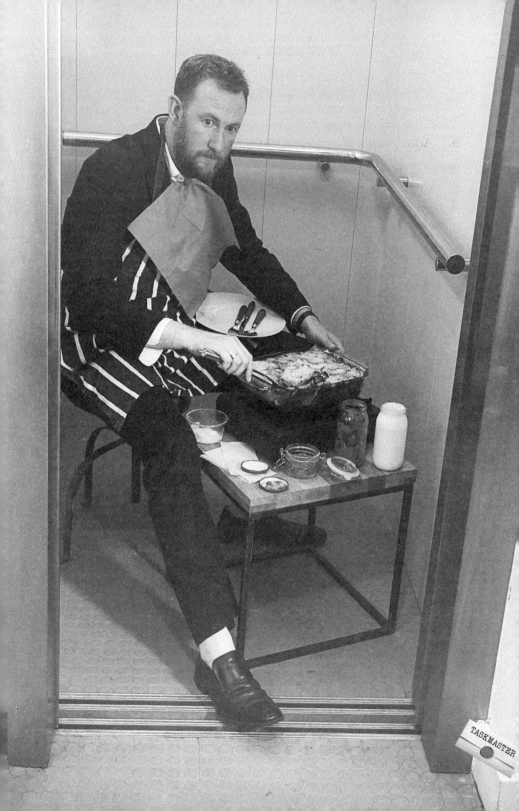

AN ABSOLUTE CASSEROLE

Lou Sanders' Dust à la Fizz Wizz

TASK: Devise the most delicious dust (series 8, episode 9)
You have five minutes to choose your ingredients, then ten minutes to make your delicious dust and serve it in this dustpan.

Ingredients:
> Burnt Razz *magazine ash*
> Fizz wizz *(popping candy)*

Method:
1. Flambée your magazine.
2. Combine the ash with the popping candy.
3. Serve in dustpan.

Jamali Maddix's Full Day Set-Up

Task: Make the best babushka meal (series 11, episode 7)
Each course must be presented inside the previous course. You have five minutes to order your ingredients and 20 minutes to prepare your babushka meal. Best babushka meal wins.

Ingredients:
> *Tinned soup (cheapest)*
> *Tiger bread*
> *Whole cooked chicken*
> *Eggs*
> *Watermelon*
>
> *Yorkshire puddings*
> *Butter*
> *Trifle*
> *Smoked salmon*

9 / ROADKILL DOUSED IN SYRUP

Method:
1. Melt butter in a pan.
2. Fry six eggs
3. Hollow out the tiger loaf.
4. Bag up a trifle and hide it in the bread.
5. Add Yorkshire puddings.
6. Place roast chicken inside.
7. Pour soup on top.
8. Layer on salmon and eggs.
9. Serve the Full Day Set-Up.

Judi Love's Tower of Love

Task: Sculpt the most beautiful sculpture (series 13, episode 7)
Your sculpture must weigh exactly 150g and be entirely edible. You have five minutes to order your ingredients.

Ingredients:

Sweets	Strawberries
Chocolate matchsticks	Hundreds and thousands
Chocolate spread	Edible flowers

Method:
1. Check the sweets are real.
2. Spread chocolate spread over sliced strawberries.
3. Stick a matchstick into one of the strawberries and skewer strawberries and sweets onto it to make a Tower of Love.
4. Add an edible flower and continue to layer strawberries and sweets.

5. Add more matchsticks, cover the ends in chocolate spread and sprinkle over hundreds and thousands.
6. Add final flowers and sweets to make the sculpture total 150g.
7. You must now completely consume your beautiful sculpture.

Kiell Smith-Bynoe's Cowering Kenyan Bench

TASK: Make an 'adjective' 'country adjectival' 'noun' (series 15, episode 7)
You must use all these ingredients and you must also clap seven times. You have 1 minute, 21 seconds. Most accurate creation wins.

Ingredients:
Sausage
Ketchup
Bun
Mustard
Grilled onions (every strand has Nairobi written on it, but too small to be seen by the human eye)

Method:
1. Chop two buns to create two long and two small pieces.
2. Balance the sausage over the two smaller pieces of the bun.
3. Stand the longer pieces of buns upright.
4. Dip the end of the sausage in mustard.
5. Drape the grilled onions over the sausage.
6. Clap.
7. Serve your Cowering Kenyan Bench.

Sue Perkins' Surprisingly Pleasant Fish Sausages

Task: Make a sausage (series 16, episode 4)
You can only use seven ingredients, each beginning with the letters of the word 'SAUSAGE'. You have five minutes to order your ingredients and 20 minutes to prepare your sausage.

Most surprising, pleasant sausage wins.

You may not order sausages.

Your time starts now.

Ingredients:

Salmon

Anchovy

Un-alive cod

Some prawns

All the herbs

Garlic

Egg

Method:

1. Dice all the fish.
2. Pan fry.
3. Shout about how vile and horrendous it is.
4. Make into two sausages.
5. Wrap in cling film to boil one and fry the other.
6. Add herb dips to two egg cups.
7. Serve.

Weirdest Thing Anyone Has Done With Food On Taskmaster: START A CULT

In Series 9, episode 10, contestants had to 'Do the most preposterous thing with a chickpea'. Ed Gamble fell in love with his and then watched in horror as it got hit by a car, and then apparently got off with it, while Rose Matafeo had a heartbreaking funeral for hers (RIP Chick Pataki), but possibly the weirdest effort was David Baddiel's.

David decided to start a religion based around the chickpea (which was in fact God), which involved taking various members of the production crew on as his acolytes and following a star (Alex) to where the chickpea was born. He went to a nearby shop, bought a can of chickpeas for 59p, opened it up, stuck his hand in and pulled out a chickpea which he claimed was the Virgin chickpea, mother of chickpea God. No, I'm not sure either.

DID IT PAY OFF? He earned 2 points and the disdain of a local shopkeeper. So, no.

RELEVANT QUOTE: 'I knew I should have shoved [the chickpea] up my arse.' – David Baddiel, having regrets on his way to the shop

TASKMASTER HALL OF GLORY

*Highest Scorer in Solo Filmed Tasks**

NAME: Chris Ramsey

NUMBER OF POINTS IN FILMED TASKS: 100 (4.04 points per task)

SERIES: 13

SERIES POINTS: 170 (3.40 points per task)

POSITION IN SERIES: An agonisingly close second

FUN FACT: Chris Ramsey was the first contestant to come from South Shields and the second came in the very next series (Sarah Millican, series 14)

GREATEST ACHIEVEMENT: Balancing a ladder on his chin just like his dad taught him in the 'Show off' task.

LOWEST MOMENT: Pretending to fall asleep to get out of talking to Fred the Swede in Swedish.

RELEVANT QUOTE: 'No way!'

*Not including tasks in the studio or team tasks.

Edinburgh Task 8: How Did It Go?

I asked the bafflingly talented Tom Basden to put the words of my contestants to music. Imagine a softly handsome young man, strumming an old guitar and singing these verses in a higher pitch than you might expect:

Love is like a stick of rock,
You can buy it in Brighton, just like cock.

Love is like a bumblebee,
I love you David Dimbleby.

Love is like a mountain range,
But once on the other side, does your view actually change?

Love is like a taxi driver,
And pulls out without indicating.

Love is like a jehovah's witness,
She knocks at your door and you must answer.
Don't look at her askance, sir,
In the interests of politeness.

Love is like an irregular dodecahedron (twelve sides, different lengths) …
And they don't appear in the gospel of St John;
But love isn't mentioned either,
Though mentioned twice is father,
That's double the mentions of dove

9 / ROADKILL DOUSED IN SYRUP

Or eleven less than the sides
Of differing lengths that provides
The shape which in Rick's mind is love.

Love is like a pipless purple orange,
It stumps attempts to trump its rhymes,
It stymies grumps and trying times.

Love is like a f***ing butterfly ...
It makes you f***ing stop and f***ing smile and f***ing sigh.

Love is like Henning Wehn,
Es ist ein lecker oberbefehlshaber und es ist mein.

Love is like a shepherd's crook,
Held too loosely by lonely men.

Love is like a Boeing Vertol CH-47 Chinook,
Don't give it a go when you're drunk on Buckfast.

Love is like a service station waitress, spitting secretly in your $15 pancakes,
Love is also like the service station pancake mixture makers, really hot and dirty and in thrall to the union.

Love is like the giant spike you like to tie on to your trike and bike around Ike Walton Lake, Wisconsin, in the winter sun,
It is pointy and dangerous and quickly gets hot to the touch.

Love is like a Miss Millie's monster meal deal (four pieces, large chips, diet coke, small gravy) ...

It may be silly but it really feels real (four kisses, nice hips, quiet bloke going crazy).

Love is like a coat we all want to wear,
Unless it's sufficiently warm outside, then a jumper will do there.

Love is like getting your hands on the last missing sticker of your Panini World Cup sticker album,
It's bloody unbelievable and you immediately show off to your friend Simon.

Love is like passing your driving test even though you mucked up your three-point turn,
And then burying your enemy in a second-rate urn.

Love is like sweating lovely perfume and milk ...
But having lactose intolerant skin.

Love is like an old man's mouth ...
It starts so high but quickly droops south.

Love is like giant squid.

Like a lot of the musical tasks in the TV show, it turned out to be bizarrely beautiful.

EDINBURGH TASK 9
21 May 2010

Dear Competitors,

Here is your belated monthly task. It's a quickie:

WHAT FRUIT AM I HOLDING?

(In the attached photo I've hidden it with a blurry white shape — I'm not holding a blurry white shape.)

It's common sense really. Good luck.

Meanwhile, some other admin. The league table is in constant flux but the three MEN currently on the podium are (in no particular order) Mr Wozniak, Mr Hall and Mr Langford. Well done you, come on everyone else.

And if you (everyone else) do want to blag some quick points, you might well learn from Mr Watson who sent me the following message: 'I will give your son a pound, either in money or book tokens etc, for each point.'

I do, obviously, have to think of my young son first, so have decided to award Mr Watson 15 bonus points (and am waiting for a cheque — points to enter table when cheque clears). Why not follow suit?

Finally, I am still waiting for the postal addresses of Mr Wilkinson, Mr Pitcher, Mr Hall and Mr Dowdeswell. Then you can have your presents!

Thank you, competitors.

A COQUETTISH FASCINATOR

TASKMASTER AND FASHION

Obviously Greg and Alex are fashion icons, dragging black suits kicking and screaming into the 21st century. But what about the rest of the show? Here is a section dedicated to all the greatest fashion choices in *Taskmaster* – the *faux pas*, the *vrais pas* and the grey, grey, grey, grey suits of Sam Campbell.

EVOLUTION OF THE TASKMASTER OUTFIT

Fashion is a confusing beast. Today, a handmade hiking-and-writing cagoule from House of Eclair might be all the rage, but tomorrow everyone might be wearing cactus shoes from Liza Tarbuck or a James Acaster half-suit half-dress (actually, scrap that last one). In the same way, the contestants' outfits have evolved over time. Here is a look at the trends over the years.

Series 1-3

ALSO KNOWN AS: The M&S Jumper Years

CHARACTERISED BY: A drab conservatism from male contestants, favouring blue and grey sweaters with inoffensive jeans, which soon proved themselves unwieldy for certain tasks (truly terrible for hiding a pineapple on one's person, for instance).

REPRESENTATIVE: Josh Widdicombe – one of the greatest players to ever play the game, but with dark jeans and a dark jumper he could have been a stagehand at the Edinburgh Festival. At least he mixed it up on Champion of Champions (wearing a replica England 1966 football kit).

FASHION FORWARD: Some contestants broke the mould – Tim Key (series 1) wore a bright red jumpsuit that wouldn't have looked out of place in series 7, while Sara Pascoe (series 3) styled a camo shirt and combat trousers combo that at least showed she knew she wasn't on a standard panel show (although possibly her agent told her she was on *Celebrity SAS: Who Dares Wins*).

10 / A COQUETTISH FASCINATOR

OUTFIT OF THE ERA: It's slim pickings, but perhaps Joe Wilkinson's dishevelled suit reflects the style of the show – formal but chaotic, falling apart at the seams, bearing the stains and weathered bruises of everything that had come before it. And yet somehow, still just about functioning.

Series 4–5

ALSO KNOWN AS: The Advent of the Boilersuit

CHARACTERISED BY: An epiphanic understanding that this was a comedy show and that certain tasks may require contestants to jump/climb on a table/do a forward roll off a pommel horse/sadly watch a jelly fall down a pole. Suddenly jeans were out and clothes that were easy to move in were in.

REPRESENTATIVE: It's hard to look past Mel Giedroyc's iconic boilersuit in series 4 – functional, stylish, well labelled (with a little 'GIEDROYC' nametag on the front and initials on the arms). There was even a little zipper pocket for collecting wax seals. Perfect.

FASHION FORWARD: While Aisling Bea's outfit was practical (a lovely tracksuit), it also had an element of costume that would become more popular in later series. A bold green number with shiny bow tie that acted as a nod to her home country of Ireland, it was the kind of outfit that says 'I'm equally comfortable running through the house pretending to be multiple wooden spoons from the *Taken* movie as I am piloting a small boat with Alex in the front.' At all times, she kept her dignity intact.

OUTFIT OF THE ERA: It's got to go to series 4's Noel Fielding, who wore a bright yellow skeleton boilersuit. *Boosh*, but make it *Taskmaster*.

It even came in handy in the hiding task, where it transformed Noel into a tiny little banana.

Series 6–8

ALSO KNOWN AS: The Costume Years

CHARACTERISED BY: Practicality is OUT and bright neon costumes that show off your penis are IN. While boiler suits are still enjoyed by the boshiest of contestants (Kerry Godliman), the most fashionable contestants now wear the kind of thing you'd get at a high-quality joke shop and/or knock-off Hollywood film set, regardless of whether it would actually help you in a task or whether it means Rhod Gilbert and James Acaster will make fun of you throughout the team task recording days.

REPRESENTATIVE: In series 6 Tim Vine changed the game by coming in a full-blown safari explorer outfit. He finished off the outfit with oversized lapels, which managed to stymy him when one caught a hook that was vital to the task without Tim noticing. Still, what do points matter when you look this good?

FASHION FORWARD: Lou Sanders' outfit – a red jumpsuit with various customised items and hidden compartments – would later inspire other craftier efforts from contestants like Daisy May Cooper.

OUTFIT OF THE ERA: It can only be Phil Wang, who wore a bright yellow outfit to honour Bruce Lee in *Game of Death*. It was meant as a homage to one of the greatest Asian entertainers in history and also, you got to see Phil's dick and balls.

RELEVANT QUOTE: 'It doesn't matter sometimes how ornate the grandfather clock is, the pendulum draws the eye.' – Greg Davies, poetically explaining that he can't stop looking at Phil's todger

Series 9-10

ALSO KNOWN AS: Actual Fashion

CHARACTERISED BY: Some legitimately quite stylish outfits – Rose Matafeo's retro brown suit (and her brilliant studio outfits); Katherine Parkinson's toffee boilersuit, made by an independent boutique London fashion designer; Johnny Vegas' tweed suit and hat in a reference to *Peaky Blinders*, complete with pocket watch. This was the era of eclectic style – subtle looks merged seamlessly with bursts of creativity to create an aura of impossible cool. Separate from this, Ed Gamble wore double denim and it was disgusting.

FASHION FORWARD: Even the more experimental/costumey outfits, such as Mawaan Rizwan's NASA spacesuit, had an element of class. (In fairness, how could anything Mawaan wears not look stylish?)

OUTFIT OF THE ERA: All the plaudits to Daisy May Cooper, however many months pregnant, for rocking a self-made superhero outfit known as 'Achievement Woman' with gold skirt, gold cape and gold crown.

Series 11-12

ALSO KNOWN AS: The Comfort Years

CHARACTERISED BY: The pandemic pushing contestants back to their comfort clothes – from the relaxed hoodies of Jamali Maddix and Alan Davies (the latter complete with a *Simpsons* easter egg), to the informal 'kids' TV presenter' dungarees of Charlotte Ritchie.

REPRESENTATIVE: No-one summed up this 'back-to-basics' fashion trend better than Sarah Kendall, the series 11 champion, in a beautiful denim jumpsuit. Simple? Yes. Unfashionable? Absolutely not. It meant she looked on her game no matter what she was doing (tasting sugar that was supposed to be salt, taking over 20 minutes to guide two comedians onto a red dot).

FASHION FORWARD: There were still mavericks in this era, including Lee Mack, who wore an Evel Knievel-inspired outfit complete with cape and helmet, although it's worth saying that Lee ended up taking off the jacket, helmet and cape for most of the tasks. If only there had been a 'Jump 20 buses' task in series 11.

OUTFIT OF THE ERA: A difficult choice but Desiree Burch's space-themed jacket reflected the perfect marriage of cosy and stylish. This is the outfit of someone who can do it all – drink a glass of water with her mouth open, talk to her friend about rainbows on the phone, spend close to three hours throwing forks at a balloon.

Series 13–15

ALSO KNOWN AS: Maximalist High Art

CHARACTERISED BY: BOLD CHOICES. Bridget Christie is a mourning gunslinger from the Wild West! Sophie Duker is wearing an outfit inspired by an old-school Refresher! Munya Chawawa is wearing a jumpsuit with the Zimbabwe flag and a little green man on his shoulder! Dara Ó Briain is in the Irish Space Programme! *Taskmaster* is back in front of an audience and we're all going to wear the maddest clothes to celebrate!

REPRESENTATIVE: The series 15 cast – not for their task outfits which were relatively tame (apart from Kiell Smith-Bynoe's red jumpsuit and Jenny Eclair's orange number) – but for the last outfit they wore in the studio, collectively all turning up in the gaudiest Sgt. Pepper's suits you can imagine.

OUTFIT OF THE ERA: All hail the Taskmistress! In a crowded field, there was one PVC madness that has to take the win – Fern Brady's blue-green catsuit with a metallic one-piece, collar and cuffs worn on top. One of the strangest outfits ever, it was made by a fetish gear company and was so tight that, in Fern's words, if she were to poo herself, the poo would bifurcate out rather than remaining inside. Maybe don't read this book while eating.

Series 16-17

ALSO KNOWN AS: Return to Normcore

CHARACTERISED BY: Nice sensible outfits worn by total weirdos, and total weirdo outfits worn by nice sensible people. You've got Julian Clary (who has worn his fair share of PVC numbers in his time) in a lovely checkered shirt, who thinks nothing of spitting a doughnut in Alex's face. There's the very plain clothes of Sam Campbell (almost Josh Widdicombe levels of a Nice Department Store), who is also one of the strangest little men to ever appear on the show. And then you've got the kind, beautiful and sweet Nick Mohammed, who decided to dress like Dracula. For reasons that have never been made clear.

REPRESENTATIVE: Sue Perkins' outfit is similar to her comedy partner's – a nice jumpsuit that prepares her for the worst in every situation (even farting in the dark listening to her own name).

OUTFIT OF THE ERA: It's obviously Nick Mohammed and Dracula, but special mention also to the all-conquering John Robins, who dressed as Queen's Freddie Mercury in his iconic yellow jacket.

GIVE ME SOME STATS:
What is the best colour to wear on Taskmaster?

The colour you wear in your job can have a massive impact on your performance – blue is best for productivity, yellow is best for happiness and claret is best for football (go Chesham United). But is the same true in *Taskmaster*? What's the best colour to wear in the show? Will a bold bright yellow turn you into a John Robins or a Phil Wang? Read on to find out.

Most common outfit colour on the show: Black (22)

Second most common outfit colour on the show: Blue (21)

Average points per task from contestants in black: 2.96 points per task

Average points per task from contestants in blue: 3.03 points per task

Bluest series (in outfits, not swears): Series 3 (four contestants)

Bluest series (in swears, not outfits): Series 9 (primarily Ed Gamble at David Baddiel)

Series with the most black suits: Series 1 (Frank Skinner and Romesh Ranganathan)

Series with the most Draculas: Series 17 (Nick Mohammed/Dracula)

Number of champions in black: Three (Josh Widdicombe, Liza Tarbuck, Richard Herring)

10 / A COQUETTISH FASCINATOR

Number of champions in blue: Five (Rob Beckett, Bob Mortimer, Ed Gamble, Sarah Kendall, Sam Campbell)

Success rate of contestants in black: 13.6%

Success rate of contestants in blue: 23.8%

Number of contestants in red/pink: Ten

Average points score of contestants in red/pink: 2.89

Number of champions in red/pink: One (Lou Sanders)

Success rate of contestants in red/pink: 10%

Number of contestants in red/pink who tried to hop over a river: One (Sophie Willan)

Number of contestants in white/grey: Nine

Average points score of contestants in white/grey: 2.95

Number of champions in white/grey: One (Mae Martin)

Success rate of contestants in white/grey: 11.1%

Number of times Lee Mack turned up to a task in Evel Knievel costume: 30

Number of buses Lee jumped over (on camera): Zero

Number of contestants in green: Ten

Average points score of contestants in green: 2.91

Number of champions in green: One (Dara Ó Briain)

Success rate of contestants in green: 10%

Colour the two non-sabotaging contestants wore in the sabotage team task: Green

Is green the most trusting colour? Yes

Number of contestants in yellow/orange: Eight

Average points score of contestants in yellow/orange: 3.17

Number of champions in yellow/orange: Four (Noel Fielding, Kerry Godliman, Sophie Duker, John Robins)

Success rate of contestants in yellow/orange: 50%

Success rate of seeing the outline of Phil's penis in every task: 100%

Conclusion

Yellow or orange are the best colours to wear if you want to be successful, with a massive success rate of champions in those colours. But be warned, there is a danger of drawing Greg's attention in a negative way too (for every Sophie Duker, there's a Mawaan Rizwan). If you want to play it safe, consider a high-scoring blue or popping on a safari suit. They're always in fashion.

HAIR FACTS AND STATS

Ever wondered what the best hair to have is if you want to win *Taskmaster*? Or whether you should grow a moustache if you want to do well? Or do you just want to remember the time Alex had really bushy eyebrows and it disgusted all the series 17 cast? Well, good news, this section is for YOU! Here are 11 facts about hair and *Taskmaster*. NB: If you hate hair, please skip ahead to the next section.

1. Statistically, the best hair colour to have on the show is brown – brunette contestants average 3.05 points per task (and feature champions like Lou Sanders, Ed Gamble and Sam Campbell). They're just ahead of blond contestants who average 3.02 points per task, although it's worth saying there have been seven blond champions (including Katherine Ryan, Rob Beckett, Kerry Godliman and Mae Martin) compared to just four brown-haired winners. At the other end, redheads do the worst, scoring just 2.84 points per task, with Katherine Parkinson and Sophie Willan bringing the average down (although Sarah 'The Hair' Kendall did manage to win with red hair).

2. However, if you really want to do well, don't reach for the hair dye, but the razor instead. There have only been four contestants who have been bald or clean shaven (Al Murray, Tim Vine, Dara Ó Briain and Kiell Smith-Bynoe), but they have an average points per task score of 3.23, and of course boast one of the highest scoring contestants ever in their ranks in Dara.

3 Despite his status as a bald king, Dara is one of the many contestants to have brought in hair as a prize task – he brought in a grey wig for Champion of Champions which he modelled on a New Zealand beach. Others include Tim Vine, who brought in a single hair belonging to Elvis Presley, and Joe Thomas, who brought in a voucher for a single hair transplant. Ed Gamble also brought in a 'Chigata Demon' for 'Weirdest wooden thing', complete with human hair and teeth, while Morgana Robinson brought in Vic Reeves' beard hair for the 'Most ridiculous thin thing' and Jenny Eclair brought in her deceased father's hair as her 'Most heroic thing' in series 15.

4 Two contestants have brought in their *own* hair as a prize task – Alice Levine in series 6 for the 'Best hairy thing which isn't alive' brought in a ball of her own hair off a hairbrush (2 points), while Mike Wozniak brought in his hair in a mohawk (as a 'punk rock hairdo wig') for the 'Thing that makes you look the toughest' (5 points).

5 The longest hair on the show goes to Jo Brand, who showed off her eyebrow hair that goes from one eyebrow, round through the garden of the Taskmaster house and then back up to her other eyebrow, at a length of 95.5 metres. NB: Some extensions may have been used.

6 Two contestants have turned their hair into a face in the show – Sarah Kendall and John Robins. For one of Sarah's efforts where she had to look the most different in four photos taken by the same automatic camera, Sarah pushed her sizeable hair into her face and put a pair of glasses over it, as if 'a century worth of hair growth' had taken place. She ended up with 3 points. Meanwhile John used poster

10 / A COQUETTISH FASCINATOR

paint to draw Freddie Mercury into the back of his head and then performed a series of vocal warm-ups as the Queen frontman. He deservedly took home the 5 points.

7 The sneakiest use of hair on the show was Sophie Duker. In a task where contestants had to disguise one body part as another when stuck out of a shower curtain, she dressed up her hair to look like a leg. She received 5 points, incredibly only 1 point more than Judi Love, who put her hand in a shoe and pretended it was her foot.

8 The most disturbing use of hair on the show is a tie between Noel Fielding and Ardal O'Hanlon: Noel for eating some of Alex's beard hair to complete the 'Eat your exotic sandwich' task in series 4, and Ardal for drowning a mannequin with their sodden hair while giving them a rinse in a cement mixer in series 13.

9 No-one with a full beard has ever won *Taskmaster* (discounting Liza Tarbuck's fantastic Alex Horne tribute goatee in Champion of Champions 2). The best anyone with a beard has done is Guz Khan. He came just 1 point behind Morgana Robinson in series 12.

10 The only contestant with facial hair to win *Taskmaster* was Richard Herring in series 10. He sported a moustache, which may have come in handy when performing as Parker, the former American football player hiding in the bushes (Greg thought he absolutely nailed 'the mute pervert'). Overall, contestants with facial hair score an average points per task score of 2.89 – well below the average.

11 In series 6, Asim Chaudhry called Greg 'the tall motherf***er with the ivory hair' and Greg said it was the nicest thing anyone had ever said to him.

Conclusion

If you want to use hair to win, shave yourself bald, rip off your moustache and beard, draw Freddie Mercury on the back of your head, and compliment Greg's silver fox locks. And, if you have time, tuck into Alex's beard. It can't hurt.

TASKMASTER HALL OF GLORY
Lowest Scoring Contestant Ever

NAME: Roisin Conaty

SERIES POINTS: 68 (2.13 points per task)

SERIES: 1

POSITION IN SERIES: Last place

FUN FACT: Roisin Conaty named the first ever episode of *Taskmaster*, during the discussion of the 'Eat as much watermelon as possible' task. She claimed she wasn't expecting to have to dig into a watermelon – she thought there would be some kind of 'melon buffet' (the name of the episode).

GREATEST ACHIEVEMENT: Getting the Taskmaster a live mouse as a present (as she revealed he'd let it slip while drunk that he really wanted one). This effort nearly topped the tattoo Josh got of Greg's name.

LOWEST MOMENT: Attempting to push a rock to Camber Sands.

RELEVANT QUOTE: 'Down an octave!'

Edinburgh Task 9: How Did It Go?

This was another less-than-successful task that was still somehow entertaining on the night, teaching us the lesson that even when things go wrong, we should embrace the mistakes. In our TV show we don't mind when no one does well; we don't mind when things fall apart; we don't mind when things are slightly rubbish. Things have to be authentic and in real life things *are* slightly rubbish.

In the photo, I was holding a lemon. There were no tricks, no clever wordplay, just a lemon. And no one guessed it correctly.

My players' answers included cherry, lychee (x2), grape (x3), gooseberry, grapefruit, kiwi, guava, pomelo (Tim Key), bonsai rhubarb (Mike Wozniak), pawpaw (Mark Watson), kumquat, papaya and tomato. People thought about it far too hard. Jarred Christmas, for example, sent this reply:

You are an English Gentleman with the environment on his mind. The month is May, meaning a lot of homegrown British fruits are in season.

You do not strike me as someone who would have an imported fruit such as a kiwi or a mango.

That narrows it down to berries, English berries or possibly an apple. An apple would be to easy, therefore we can strike that off the list ... But you are a tricky fellow, therefore going for an obvious fruit like the apple could be an elaborate double bluff.

But you also have a beard and statistically men with beards are prone to the triple bluff, thus I can deduce that in your hand is no apple at all.

Back to the berries ... black, rasp, straw, blue, red whortle, goose or even the berry cousin, the currant. I think you have the same opinion as me when it comes to currants ... they are a poor man's berry and therefore bullshit. So in your hand is no currant.

The berries then ... a red whortle is too weird, a goose too funny, a blackberry too racist, a raspberry too messy, a blueberry too smurfy.

I deduce that you have in your confident hand a STRAWBERRY!

Unless you have an orange.

My final answer though is apple.

Jarred

Zero points, Jarred. The real winner of the task was our singer Tom Basden, who guessed that I was holding an egg.

EDINBURGH TASK 10
4 June 2010

Evening all,

Thanks for your fruit guesses. If you didn't submit one, you've got 24 hours in which to do so (a bit like the programme *24* – deadlines, cliffhangers, guessing etc).

But now on to this month's task!

HALF AN HOUR IN HONG KONG

On 20 June I am going to Hong Kong for six days. Please tell me what to do when I'm there by suggesting an activity that takes no more than half an hour. Just tell me where to go and what to do. The more details the better.

YOU MUST SEND ME YOUR SUGGESTION IN THE NEXT TWO WEEKS. SO YOU MIGHT AS WELL GET ON AND DO IT NOW(ish).

I will attempt to try all the activities suggested (or at least the top ten), and the ones I enjoy most (for whatever reasons) will win the suggester the points.

Good luck.

Horne

(The Taskmaster)

EMERGENCY TASK
16 June 2010

First person to send me a photo (by email, mobile, post or hand) of themselves holding an egg will win FIVE POINTS and a DISTINCT ADVANTAGE in a special bonus task that will commence on Friday.

So send me a picture of yourself holding an egg NOW.

Good luck.

Meanwhile, I'm off to Hong Kong on Sunday (not with family, as some of you were wondering), so get your suggestions in for how I should spend half an hour asap.

Bye!

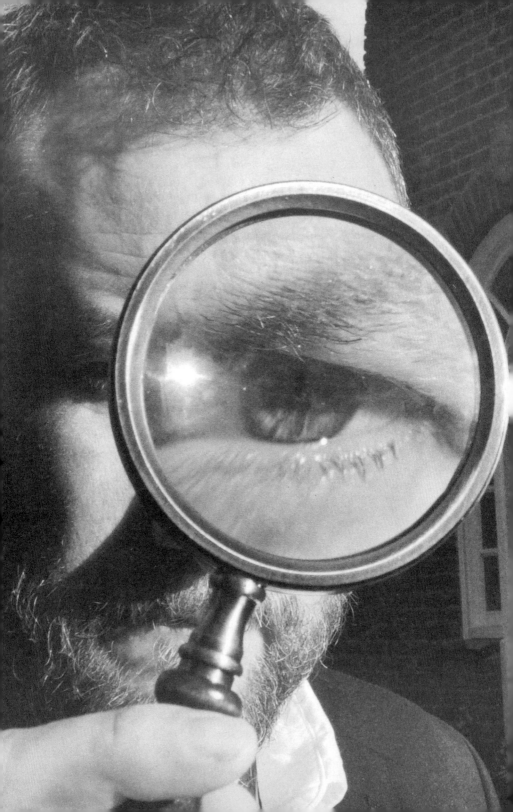

ENORMOUS HUGENESS

TASKMASTER AND CELEBRITY

Taskmaster is well up on its celebrity culture. Yes, there's nothing we enjoy more than logging on to celebritysizes.com and comparing them to our own weights. That's why we've got this section here – to celebrate the people from outside the show who deign to come in to brighten up our lives. Even if they are f***ing nightmares.

OTHER HUMANS FEATURED ON TASKMASTER

Occasionally the show throws contestants a curveball by forcing them to interact with a member of the general public. This section celebrates these tireless and selfless citizens, who give up their valuable time to be a part of the stupidest television show currently on air. Thank you.

Rosalind

TASK: Write and perform a song about a stranger

EPISODE: Series 5, episode 8 ('Their Water's So Delicious')

ROLE: To answer a series of questions about herself and then listen to two wildly differing songs written and performed by the contestants.

HOW SHE GOT ON THE SHOW: She answered an advert asking whether she wanted to have a comic song written about her, and the rest was history.

NOTABLE MOMENTS: Too many to mention – Bob Mortimer asking 'Should we strike you?' as soon as he entered the room, then what's her favourite meat and then whether or not she had ever stolen anything. Mark Watson and Nish Kumar getting distracted by a tree midway through their song about her. The set blowing over during Aisling Bea, Bob Mortimer and Sally Phillip's song while Rosalind sat happily in a deck chair; Mark and Nish cowering in fear of the wrath of Alan.

FUN FACTS: There was a third verse in Aisling, Bob and Sally's song about Rosalind – 'Quite Good Considering' – that was cut

11 / ENORMOUS HUGENESS

for time. It involved a flying lesson that didn't go too well and an ex-flame who broke Rosalind's heart. The original chorus ('Rosalind's a nightmare') was actually 'Rosalind's a bitch' but was changed just before the performance (not at Rosalind's request – she quite enjoyed it).

RELEVANT QUOTES ABOUT HER: 'I'm always seeing you do cool stuff. I try my best but it's never … good enough.' – Mark and Nish 'Rosalind's a f***ing nightmare.' – Aisling, Bob and Sally

Councillor Peter Hudson, AKA the Mayor of Chesham

TASK: Impress this Mayor

EPISODE: Series 2, episode 3 ('A Pistachio Eclair')

ROLE: To judge the contestants' attempts to impress him.

HOW HE GOT ON THE SHOW: Alex met him at a charity football match and was inspired to rewrite a task for him.

NOTABLE MOMENTS: Receiving 42 Calippos from Joe Wilkinson; listening to a homemade rap by Katherine Ryan; looking at a pistachio eclair Jon Richardson had found on the Internet.

FUN FACT: Peter ate one of Joe Wilkinson's Calippos and kept another in his freezer for posterity.

RELEVANT QUOTES ABOUT HIM: 'A volunteer but that's not all/Three kids but just one came from his balls/That's Peter Hudson, you know that you can trust him, yeah.' – Katherine Ryan's rap for Peter Hudson

Hugh the Gentleman

TASK: Find out what this gentleman did for a living. You must whisper at all times. The gentleman can only nod or shake his head. The gentleman can only lie.

EPISODE: Series 3, episode 4 ('A Very Nuanced Character')

ROLE: To nod and shake his head enthusiastically at a series of increasingly frustrated whispered questions from the contestants.

HOW HE GOT ON THE SHOW: Despite what Greg said, he is not Alex's dad, but has a family connection with producer Andy Cartwright.

NOTABLE MOMENTS: Rob Beckett gasping in his face when he discovered he worked for the NHS; Sara Pascoe asking him if he makes babies in a test tube.

RELEVANT QUOTES ABOUT HIM: 'Is everyone getting someone dressed up as their future self?' – Dave Gorman, who was wearing nearly the exact same clothes as Hugh

Jennifer Christine Wright

TASK: Create the best caricature of the person on the other side of the curtain

EPISODE: Series 4, episode 1 ('A Fat Bald White Man')

ROLE: To sit and answer 'yes' and 'no' questions, while contestants attempted to find out what they looked like without looking at them.

HOW SHE GOT ON THE SHOW: The age-old method of looking for 'supporting artists' on the internet and casting someone who was thought to be right for the role.

11 / ENORMOUS HUGENESS

NOTABLE MOMENTS: When Hugh Dennis worked out the hack of using a mirror to discover what Jennifer looked like and then drew the worst picture of the five contestants.

RELEVANT QUOTES ABOUT HER: 'From you what we've learnt, Hugh, is that the mirror image turns a black woman to a fat, bald, white man.' – Greg Davies on Hugh's drawing

Geoff, the Former Traffic Warden

TASK: Cheer up this former traffic warden

EPISODE: Series 7, episode 5 ('Lotta Soup')

ROLE: To be grumpy in front of the contestants, who had to attempt to cheer him up.

HOW HE GOT ON THE SHOW: Another family connection from producer Andy Cartwright: Geoff is Andy's father-in-law and, since appearing on the show, has had two lovely new knees.

NOTABLE MOMENTS: James Acaster making Geoff go 'mountain-climbing' (walk up a ladder) in 'Tenerife' (the Taskmaster garden) with his 'wife' (Alex); Kerry Godliman singing 'If You're Happy and You Know It' at Geoff to no response; Jess trying fake-laughing in Geoff's face, again to no response.

FUN FACT: Alex Horne is not actually Geoff's wife.

RELEVANT QUOTES ABOUT HIM: 'Are you ticklish, Geoff?' – Kerry Godliman, before tickling Geoff's sore knees

Carol

TASK: Find out what you have in common with this person

EPISODE: Series 6, episode 8 ('What Kind of Pictures?')

ROLE: To have a conversation in a nice pub with the contestants, who are trying to find how many remarkable things they have in common with her.

HOW SHE GOT ON THE SHOW: She and her husband knew Alex and his wife years previously from regular meetings in a coffee shop in Chesham.

NOTABLE MOMENTS: Russell Howard asking her if she likes ear wax removal videos (and then showing her one); Asim Chaudhry asking her if she had won a BAFTA.

FUN FACT: Carol has not watched an ear wax removal video since then. And while she hasn't won a BAFTA, she did win a gold medal for ballroom dancing.

RELEVANT QUOTES ABOUT HER: 'I'm beginning to think that Carol's just a nice lady who'll agree to anything.' – Greg Davies, on whether or not Carol actually enjoyed the ear wax removal video

Gareth Simon Kalyan, the Magician

TASK: Get to know this person. You will be tested on your knowledge of this person in ten minutes' time

EPISODE: Series 9, episode 5 ('Another Spoon')

ROLE: To lie, tell the truth and brag as the contestants asked him questions. Also make his tongue really, really big.

11 / ENORMOUS HUGENESS

HOW HE GOT ON THE SHOW: Alex knew a friend of Gareth's in the Magic Circle, and asked if he had any recommendations for a magician for the show. Gareth had also been in a homemade version of *Taskmaster* for people exclusively in the Magic Circle (really), which Alex had seen and enjoyed.

NOTABLE MOMENTS: When Katy Wix went off script and asked if he had ever needed any therapy or if he got on well with his parents; Jo Brand asking if he'd ever been to Penge.

GREATEST FEAR: Being plonked right in the middle of the deep ocean.

FUN FACT: Gareth has still not been to Penge, but was approached by a Penge hotel offering him a stay off the back of this episode.

RELEVANT QUOTES: 'My best trick is a stage trick where I end up taking my clothes off. I'm on stage wearing women's underwear.' – Gareth Simon Kalyan. 'Is that a brag?' – Jo Brand; 'It's a strange brag.' – David Baddiel

Quentin

TASK: Correctly guess this person's name

EPISODE: Series 13, episode 6 ('The 75th Question')

ROLE: To answer many, many, many 'yes' and 'no' questions from the contestants, ostensibly about the contestant's first name but frequently entirely unrelated.

HOW HE GOT ON THE SHOW: Another family connection, this time the father-in-law of Gabby Tomlinson (*Taskmaster's* assistant producer, skateboarding granny and sausage cement mixer operator).

AN ABSOLUTE CASSEROLE

NAMES THAT WERE GUESSED BEFORE QUENTIN: Andrew, Pimpernickel, Luigi, Quantum, Leonardo, Xavier, Barrick, Tiger, Obama, Zebedee, Shakespeare, Maximus, Vlad, Ludwig, Quinney, Quasimodo, Quantus, Quiz.

NUMBER OF QUESTIONS IT TOOK THE CONTESTANTS TO GET THE NAME RIGHT: 75

FUN FACT: There was actually a giant Q hidden on the stage which may have provided a clue to the contestants if they had noticed.

RELEVANT QUOTES: 'Are you a French trapeze artist?' – Ardal O'Hanlon, setting the tone with the first question of the night; 'What sort of f***ing opener was that?!' – Greg Davies

TASKMASTER HALL OF GLORY

Highest Scoring Contestant in Solo Tasks

NAME: Dara Ó Briain

SERIES POINTS: 184 (3.68 points per task)

SERIES: 14

POSITION IN SERIES: First, despite Sarah Millican's best efforts

FUN FACTS: Dara has won more solo tasks than anyone else in the show – 17. He scored 5 points in 39.53 per cent of his solo tasks, the highest percentage ever. Dara also scored 43 in live tasks, winning six out of seven of the live solo tasks (the highest tally ever).

GREATEST ACHIEVEMENTS: Scoring 30 points in a single episode; catching a baby in a deckchair while drinking a martini; getting through the team tasks without throttling John Kearns.

LOWEST MOMENT: Let's just say 'milk and microwaves' and leave it at that.

RELEVANT QUOTE: 'Wait, what?'

ANIMALS AND CHILDREN

There are three golden rules in show business. 1: Never work with animals. 2: Never work with children. 3: Never get on the wrong side of noted fork and marble salesman Qrs Tuvwxyz. *Taskmaster* has broken all three. Here's a look at some of the most egregious examples of the first two.

Nell the toddler

TASK: Make the best thing to engage a toddler

EPISODE: Series 8, episode 4 ('The Barrel Dad')

ROLE: To be engaged by the very strange toys that the contestants had created for her.

HOW SHE GOT ON THE SHOW: Nell is the daughter of series producer Andy Cartwright and she was paid £50 for her time.

NOTABLE MOMENTS: Receiving a giant mallet and duck from Lou Sanders with a song telling her to 'hit the ducky on the head'; becoming mesmerised by Paul Sinha's toy of a small baking tray of water and some threshing sharks.

FUN FACTS: Andy has since revealed that if she were to judge the tasks again (this time when she was five), she would have picked Joe Thomas as the winner – potentially changing *Taskmaster* scoring history forever. Nell was referenced in a later task in series 12, when a rolling sports news graphic revealed that 'Breaking Nell' would go up against 'Ducky' once more at the C&G Arena.

11 / ENORMOUS HUGENESS

RELEVANT QUOTES ABOUT THEM: 'I'm not sure that Nell was 100 per cent on top of your narrative.' – Greg Davies on Paul's threshing shark story

Marco the cute dog

TASK: Make a cute toy for a cute dog
EPISODE: Series 12, episode 6 ('A Chair in a Sweet')
ROLE: To play with the cute toys that the contestants had provided for him (which ranged from a series of pipes that Alan Davies called 'Pipey', to Desiree Burch's tennis ball monstrosity 'Chonky', to some roast chicken from Morgana Robinson).
BREED: Rough coat Jack Russell Terrier
HOW HE GOT ON THE SHOW: Animals on TV, including humans, have to be treated properly so you can't just allow any dog onto the show. Marco came with television experience and an excellent animal handler, and was chosen because of his personality, appearance and gravitas.
NOTABLE MOMENTS: Becoming entirely infatuated with 'Priscilla', Guz Khan's confusing toy made from 'string, a tongue and some toilet rolls' (in Alex's words), to the point that Alex had to usher Marco out of the room at the end of the five minutes.
RELEVANT QUOTES: 'Is it a boy dog or a lady dog? Imagine if it's a boy dog in heat and we made a lady dog.' – Guz Khan, coming up with the concept of Priscilla for Marco

Flossie

TASK: Convince a child you're asleep

EPISODE: Series 16, episode 8 ('Never Packed a Boot')

ROLE: To assess whether or not the contestants pretending to be asleep were actually asleep.

HOW THEY GOT ON THE SHOW: Flossie is a friend of one of Alex's nieces and Flossie's mum is a friend of one of Alex's sister-in-laws.

CONTROVERSIAL MOMENT: She guessed everyone correctly apart from Susan Wokoma, which makes sense because she's a great actor, and Sam Campbell, which made less sense, because he's not a great actor and he'd put a plastic flamingo in his bed. Later on it was revealed that Sam had offered her £100 to say he was asleep, in an act of brazen match-fixing that would make Dave Gorman blush. Greg allowed it though, and Sam took the 5 points.

DID SAM PAY FLOSSIE THE MONEY: Yes, in book tokens.

RELEVANT QUOTES: 'Would Sam actually give me £100?' – Flossie, having a crisis of morals

FACTS ABOUT EGGS 5

🥚 In a task where contestants had to play golf with eggs, Romesh Ranganathan (a vegan) used a staggering 36 eggs (to the point that the show ran out of eggs). He believed he could play the game without breaking eggs. He was wrong.

🥚 The biggest single cell organism in the world is an ostrich egg. On average it is 15 centimetres long and 12 centimetres across.

🥚 The words 'eggs benedict' do not sound anything like 'Greg Davies', despite what Nick Mohammed/Dracula has been telling you.

🥚 Storing eggs upside down makes them last longer.

🥚 There were six egg puns in Steve Pemberton's adventurous egg journey – the protagonist was 'Eggbert Nobacon', his goat was called Shelley, he was going down Albumen Alley in the town of Yolkstone, avoiding the Omelette Express and nearly crashing at Crackatoa Falls. He received 0 points, because he smashed his egg right at the end.

NEW YEAR'S TREAT STATS

For the uninitiated, every New Year the Taskmaster house opens its doors to the rich and the famous, inviting them in to humiliate themselves on a one off special for national TV. There have been national treasures, politicians, Olympians, film stars, *Strictly Come Dancing* judges and John Kearns' mate from university. Here are some of the essential stats for the New Year's Treats.

Youngest contestant: Lenny Rush (NYT 4) – 14 years old

Oldest contestant: Deborah Meaden (NYT 4) – 64 years old

Most gold Olympic medals: ~~Rylan Clark~~ Sir Mo Farah (NYT 3) – four medals

Most gold Paralympic medals: Jonnie Peacock (NYT 2) – two medals

Highest net worth: Deborah Meaden – £50 million

Most '*Guardian* Album of the Year' awards: Rebecca Lucy Taylor (NYT 3) – one award

Most MOBO awards: Lady Leshurr (NYT 1) – three awards

Highest scoring contestant: Adrian Chiles (NYT 2) – 22

Lowest scoring contestant: Claudia Winkleman (NYT 2) – 6 points

Highest scoring contestant in objectively judged tasks: Adrian Chiles – 10 (5.00 points per task)

11 / ENORMOUS HUGENESS

Lowest scoring contestant in objectively judged tasks: Claudia Winkleman – 1 (0.50 points per task)

Highest scoring contestant in subjectively judged tasks: Kojey Radical (NYT 4) – 10 (5.00 points per task)

Lowest scoring contestant in subjectively judged tasks: Claudia Winkleman – 5 (1.67 points per task)

Highest proportion of points scored in the studio (as opposed to in the house): Nicola Coughlan (NYT 1) – 70%

Lowest proportion of points scored in the studio (as opposed to in the house): John Hannah (NYT 1) – 0%

Most inconsistent contestants: Rylan Clark (NYT 1) and Kojey Radical (won two tasks, came last in two tasks)

Most expensive prize task: Carol Vorderman's customised 'military' vehicle with working electric roof and compostable toilet (NYT 3), cost £XXXXXX (redacted on order of the British Armed Forces)

Least expensive prize task: Amelia Dimoldenberg's cardboard fly coffin, complete with sticker (NYT 3), cost £X (redacted out of taste)

Most disappointing prize task: John Hannah's Bobbit, because it ruined the illusion of Hollywood glamour for Greg

Least age-appropriate gift: Lenny Rush (14 years old) bringing in beer* and cigarettes**

*It was squash really
It was a cigar really*
***Not really – candy cigarettes

Most dead person brought in for a prize task: Nicola Coughlan bringing in a skeleton

Most middle fingers flashed at Alex for a catty comment: Claudia Winkleman – one (deserved)

Most lollypop men sworn at: Rylan Clark – one (partially deserved)

Best at receiving head massages from Alex: Sir Mo Farah

Best at yelling 'Whoooo' outside the Taskmaster House: Sir Mo Farah

Most poppadoms fed menacingly to Alex: Kojey Radical

Most T-shirts made commemorating the most poppadoms fed menacingly to Alex Horne: Kojey Radical

GIVE ME SOME STATS:
What profession is the best at New Year's Treat?

Sportspeople (including dancers) have an average points-per-task score of 3.47 in New Year's Treat, with the highest scorer being NYT 2023 champion Sir Mo Farah (4.00 points per task). However, it's worth saying it's a small sample size (just three of the twenty NYT contestants so far have been sportspeople or dancers).

By contrast, journalists and presenters score just 2.70 points per task, although that score is predominantly pulled down by Claudia Winkleman, who scored just 1.20 points per task (but she had a nice time throwing an egg over a cow so that's all that matters).

Slightly below the journalists are the actors and musicians, who come in at just 2.63 points per task. The only actor/musician to win a New Year's Treat is Lenny Rush, who scored 19 points at 3.80 points per task.

The assorted rest (politicians, naturalists, businesspeople) score 2.93, with Steve Backshall coming the closest to victory in NYT 4, scoring 18 points (3.60 points per task). But it wasn't a waste of time for Deborah Meaden. She now knows that standard toasters are not voice-activated, so you don't have to yell 'GO DOWN' for them to work.

Edinburgh Task 10: How Did It Go?

We've never been abroad in the TV show. We sometimes daydream of tasks set on desert islands or in Iceland or space, but instead we end up in train museums and disused nightclubs.

This trip to Hong Kong did yield enough funny and fascinating task attempts to make me still hold on to our dream of tasking in foreign fields. Who wouldn't want to witness the following instructions being carried out?

Joe Wilkinson told me to go to a British pub and have a pint of traditional British beer; while Henning Wehn sent me to: GERMAN SAUSAGE KING; G/F, Southorn Centre, 2 O'Brien Road, Wan Chai, Hong Kong; and Lloyd Langford instructed me to buy some earrings in Kowloon's jade market for his girlfriend (Anne Edmonds, star of *Taskmaster Australia* season 2).

Lloyd Woolf issued these commands:

- Stay in the lift in your hotel.*
- Up and down, for half an hour.
- Try and sell something on your person – some of your clothes, something out of your pocket – to everyone who gets in.** That's my suggestion.

* If there's no lift in your hotel, find a different one. Like in a big shopping mall.
** If there's an adult there, like a bellboy, who seems to disapprove, move on to another lift.

11 / ENORMOUS HUGENESS

Yes, these were memorable times for the fledgling Taskmaster's assistant and I undertook every suggestion, with my own sidekick, Tim Key. But undoubtedly the most memorable (Tim played the part of my wife, obviously) was put forward by Stuart Goldsmith and I highly recommend you all do this at some point in some place:

- This mission is to be undertaken with a friend, perhaps your wife. You haven't mentioned Hong Kong on your gig-list so I'm going to assume it's a holiday.
- Wear some shoes with laces. You're an Englishman abroad so this shouldn't be a problem.
- Collect cutlery from your hotel, say five or six pieces of different sizes. Maybe a very large spoon as well. Ask your friend/wife to carry them.
- Purchase a grill shelf, the slidey bit that goes into an oven that you'd maybe rest a baking tray on.
- You could, for example, find one here: Pantry Magic, kitchen suppliers at 5 Lok Ku Rd, located near the Man Mo Temple, just below Hollywood Road.
- But you could equally borrow one from your hotel. That might be fun and inexpensive.
- Go to The Avenue of the Stars in Tsim Sha Tsui, Victoria Harbour.
- (Sub-adventure: find the star that represents Jackie Chan and send me a picture of you next to it, doing an arguably racist kung-fu pose).

AN ABSOLUTE CASSEROLE

- Remove your shoelaces and tie one each to the top left and right corners of the grill shelf.
- Leaving about two foot of lace above each corner. Wrap the very ends of your laces about three times round your index fingers. Secure the ends of the wrapped laces with each thumb, so they don't slip off. You can do this yourself or ask your wife to help you.
- Put your index fingers as deep into your ears as is comfortable. Left finger goes in the left ear, etc.
- Lean forwards at an angle of about 15–20 degrees and review your situation – the grill shelf should now be suspended by your shoelaces, which are wrapped around your fingers which are sticking into your ears. The grill shelf should be dangling freely and not brushing against your body. If this is not an accurate description of your situation, review the steps above. Ask your wife to help you.
- Look out at the breathtaking view of the harbour, as your wife rattles and bangs the cutlery she's been carrying against the suspended grill shelf, and the sound waves resonate via the laces, directly into your inner ears and mind.

Wow!

Now let your wife have a go. She can probably use your laces rather than remove her own.

And that's the Inner Ear Orchestra – Cantopop Edition.

11 / ENORMOUS HUGENESS

STOP PRESS

Before Task 11 I issued an emergency task, to keep people on their toes. It was simply this:

- Hold an egg.
- Fastest wins.

Again, Tim Key emerged victorious, grabbing one even quicker than he'd snatched that hedgehog (according to his text message). But of more interest is the fact that Tom Basden sent me a selfie of him holding a lemon.

EDINBURGH TASK 11
4 July 2010

Afternoon Taskmen (and Josie),

It's July. We're almost there. August next (remember, you're all invited to the big results reveal: Edinburgh Pleasance Queen Dome, just after midnight on Friday, 27 August. And you can bring as many comps as you like. In fact, if you could let me know if you think you can make it, that'd be very helpful).

Meanwhile, this month's task:

WHERE'S ALLY?

On a particular day this month I will be at a particular place at a particular time. First three people to find me get the points (15 for first, 10 for second, 5 for third). That's it.

I will only tell you where I am on the morning of that particular day. Then it's a race. I know some of you will find it harder to get there than others (Mr Pitcher, for example, will probably be in Sweden — I will probably not be in Sweden). That's a shame.

So, see you in this particular location on a particular day this month.

Good luck.

On your marks, get set ... wait.

THEN 20 JULY – TO MARK OLVER

Dear Mark,

Due to the fact that you live outside London I have decided to give you an extra couple of days warning as to my whereabouts for this month's challenge.

So you are hereby warned that this Saturday, 24 July, I shall be at London Zoo (probably near the giraffes). If you find me there you shall receive many, many points.

I hope that happens.

Yours,

The Taskmaster

A SHOW ABOUT PEDANTRY

TASKMASTER AND LANGUAGE

Many different languages have been featured on *Taskmaster* – the English language, the Swedish language, love language (every time Alex talks to Greg), hate language (every time Greg talks to Alex). Here's a section tangentially related to language in *Taskmaster*!

A SHORT STORY INVOLVING FIFTY TASKMASTER CONTESTANTS

On the thirteenth day of Christmas, Alex wanted to get Greg a present. He'd already got him the 364 items listed in the first 12 festive days, so it was time to get the next birds on the list: 13 brown peacocks. A niche hue, of course, but that's what the Taskmaster wanted.

Time was of the essence, so Alex would have to gamble and rob one from the zoo. Of course, if he was caught, he'd be thrown in prison. He would not pass go. But, mark my words, this was a risk he was prepared to take.

A little nervous about nicking one, Alex needed the loo so popped into a nearby Starbucks. The door was locked. 'Only for customers,' he was told. He tried his own key, but it was the wrong brand. Alex's blood boiled, although that might have just been because he was hungry, so the assistant decided to kill two birds with one stone and head for a ruby murray instead. He filled up with a rogan josh with extra chillis followed by a Kendal mint cake, a lolly and a raisin eclair. Quite a meal, ja?

Sated, and to be frank, rather too full, Alex sallied forth to the zoo and found the relevant enclosure. Trying to be sneaky, he barely rustled the ferns and daisies, neglected to swing on a vine (a French vine) and bobbed down. So far, so good. He took a breath, then rose up to see … robins. No brown peacocks.

What he did see was a zookeeper, 'Anne' written on her name badge, who was fishing with a rod and a caster off a bridge: 'Hey!' said Alex. 'What?' said Anne. 'Can I ask you something?' said Alex.

12 / A SHOW ABOUT PEDANTRY

'I'm happy fielding any questions!' said Anne. 'OK', said Alex, 'any chance I could buy 13 brown peacocks off you? I can pay you in pounds, sterling.'

There was silence. 'Will Anne help?' thought Alex.

'It's a great spot for herrings!' said Anne.

This was appalling. The carol didn't feature herrings! They were only in the 'Second Noel'. Alex knew this because he was a godly man. But Anne was a guru. She threw a herring up into the air and lo, 13 brown peacocks swooped in and plucked the fish from the air before landing in Alex's net.

He paid the zookeeper, snuck them out of the front gates and back to Greg. 'This will do,' he said when he saw them. And Alex was pleased. Peace be with you.

FACTS ABOUT EGGS 6

🥚 Across the 17 series and various specials, the word 'egg' has been mentioned on *Taskmaster* 822 times. This is known as a 'Taskmaster's Dozen'.

🥚 If you bought this many eggs, it would cost you between £274 and £431.55, depending on the quality of egg you bought and/or your ability to haggle.
(NB: if you are Phil Wang, it will cost considerably more.)

🥚 The purported fastest egg eater in the world is Josh Cottreau, lead singer of Australian punk rock band Fangz, who *claims* to have eaten 143 eggs in under four minutes. If Mr Cottreau is to be believed, and if he could keep his EERPM (egg eating rate per minute) up, it would take him 22 minutes and 59.4 seconds to eat the amount of eggs mentioned in *Taskmaster*.

🥚 If you lined up 822 eggs vertically next to St Paul's Cathedral, they would reach nearly halfway up, although you would probably be stopped and cautioned by the police before you got anywhere near two dozen eggs, à la Tim Vine at Bristol Airport.

SUSIE DENT'S INVOLVEMENT

There are times when the wording of a task can be so mind-boggling that it baffles the brains of mere mortals like Alex Horne. When this happens, he has no choice but to get some outside help from everyone's favourite wordsmith and star of Channel 4's *Countdown*, Susie Dent, to arbitrate.

Dent decision 1: The 'Yoga ball' task

TASK WORDING: Place three exercise balls on the yoga mat on top of the hill. The task is complete when all three balls sit fully inflated and stationary on the mat. Fastest wins. Your time starts now.

EPISODE: Series 2, episode 1 ('Fear of Failure')

WHAT HAPPENED: While everyone else struggled to the top of the hill (particularly Jon Richardson, given his little legs), Richard Osman read the task a different way, seeing 'on top of the hill' as a descriptor of where the yoga mat currently was, rather than a location that he had to place the balls. So, rather than taking the balls to the top of the hill, he brought the mat down to the bottom and put the balls on top of it. Task complete.

SUSIE SAID: The task was 'open to interpretation' and that Richard's interpretation of it was 'unusual, but not impossible'.

RELEVANT QUOTES: 'I know Susie and she has had a few too many of [*mimes drinking beer*]. If she read that in the evening, I would discount it.' – Joe Wilkinson

Dent decision 2: The 'Negative bell' task

TASK WORDING: Make and wear a popcorn necklace with at least five pieces of popcorn and then do the opposite of the following:
- You must under no circumstances not avoid not making the bell not ring.
- The task is over when you have either rung the bell or not rung the bell and said 'I did the right thing' three times.
- Fastest to not do the wrong thing wins.
- If you don't do the right thing, you lose five points.

Your time started when you started reading the task.

EPISODE: Series 12, episode 8 ('A Couple of Ethels')

WHAT HAPPENED: Four out of five of the contestants panicked over the double negatives, while Victoria Coren Mitchell got fixated on threading the popcorn onto the sewing needle. Alan Davies, Morgana Robinson and Guz Khan all rang the bell (although as this task was set in a desecrated church, Guz was more worried about the threat of a couple of ghost nuns called Ethel cursing him), while Desiree Burch and Victoria weren't.

SUSIE SAID: This is my thinking. There are five 'negatives', so it comes out as equivalent to 'make the bell not ring'. 'Not making the bell not ring' is a double negative and comes to the same thing as 'making the bell ring'. 'Not avoid' is double negative that renders itself redundant, so you end up with 'You must under no circumstances make the bell ring.'

BUT THEN: Alex asked if she'd included the first line – do the opposite of the following. And she hadn't.

ALEX'S NICKNAMES

Little Alex Horne has been called many things on the show over the years, most of them unprintable. Here are some of the best.

- The Admiral of Administration (series 4, episode 2)
- Beta Male Assistant (series 4, episode 3)
- Extremely Dependent Adjudicator (series 5, episode 3)
- Furry Little Friend (series 5, episode 4)
- My Impersonal Assistant (series 6, episode 1)
- The Naughty Boy (series 4, episode 7)
- The Blob of Mayonnaise That's Dripped out of Your Sandwich Onto Your Trousers, Remaining a Nagging Reminder of All the Clumsy Mistakes in Life You've Ever Made (series 6, episode 4)
- My Hypoallergenic Fuzzball of an Assistant (series 7, episode 2)
- My Pint-sized PA (series 7, episode 3)
- A Rancorous Pustule of a Human Being That Happens To Be Very Good at Microsoft Excel (series 7, episode 7)
- My Quasi Quartermaster (series 7, episode 9)
- A Scruffy, Lice-Infested Baby Rat (series 8, episode 4)
- A Boy With Wonky Teeth That I Hate (series 8, episode 5)
- A Complete Arsehole (by Tina Turner, series 9, episode 2)
- A Long Human Rat (series 9, episode 3)
- A Man Who, Naked, Looks Like a Weird Ill Monkey (series 9, episode 4)

AN ABSOLUTE CASSEROLE

- What You Get if You Throw Fox Hair at a Cylinder of Meat (series 9, episode 6)
- A Man Who, Without Hair, Is As Physically Featureless As One Sausage (series 9, episode 8)
- A Pipe-Cleaner Crossed With a Weasel (series 9, episode 10)
- A Jittery Feral Man With a Bearded Protuberance He Calls a Face (series 10, episode 4)
- The Human Woolly Kebab (series 10, episode 5)
- A Saveloy That's Been Tossed Around by a Moulting Dog (series 10, episode 9)
- A Human Pencil With a Killer Smile (series 11, episode 3)
- A Hairy Cylinder of Subservience (series 11, episode 7)
- This Hairy Tube (series 11, episode 9)
- My Biological Son (series 11, episode 10)
- A Weird Victorian Clockwork Toy Soldier (series 12, episode 3)
- The Answer to the Question 'What Happens When You Throw Chunks of Pork at a Revolving Car-wash Brush?' (series 12, episode 8)
- The Blow-Dried Otter (series 12, episode 9)
- A Baffled Hare (series 13, episode 6)
- The Antithesis of a Champion (Champion of Champions 2)
- A Wretched Hairy Weasel (series 14, episode 2)
- A Really Boring Chemistry Teacher Crossed With Another Really Boring Chemistry Teacher (series 14, episode 8)
- What a Corpse Looks Like After the Hair Continues to Grow Post Mortem (series 15, episode 4)

12 / A SHOW ABOUT PEDANTRY

- Friendless Oddball (series 16, episode 1)
- A Poodle Who Just About Escaped a House Fire on His Hind Legs (series 17, episode 6)
- A Giant Revolving Kebab That a Kid in Bottom-set Art Has Drawn a Face On (series 17, episode 10)

Nicknames not given by Greg

- The Little F***er (by Morgana Robinson, series 12, episode 1)
- Bandana Guy (by himself, series 5, episode 6)
- A Different Man (by Liza Tarbuck, series 6, episode 10)
- Filthy Little Ferret (an erotic *Taskmaster* fanfic author on the Internet, as mentioned in series 15, episode 3)

WORDSMITHS – EPISODE TITLE GENIUSES

Some contestants might not be the best at throwing or jumping or dancing, or remembering not to take the banana out of the lab in tasks where you've specifically been told you can't take the banana out of the lab. But what these contestants lack in points, they sometimes more than make up for in their ability to coin an episode title. Here are the contestants who are the best at naming eps.

Liza Tarbuck

SERIES: 6 and Champion of Champions 2

NUMBER OF TITLES: Five

NAMES OF EPISODES: 'Tarpeters' (series 6, episode 2); 'BMXing!' (series 6, episode 4); 'What Kind of Pictures?' (series 6, episode 8); 'He Was a Different Man' (series 6, episode 10); 'The Alpine Darling' (Champion of Champions 2)

Mike Wozniak

SERIES: 11

NUMBER OF TITLES: Five (possibly four)

NAMES OF EPISODES: 'It's Not Your Fault' (series 11, episode 1); 'The Lure of The Treacle Puppies'* (series 11, episode 2); 'Premature Conker' (series 11, episode 4); 'Absolute Casserole' (series 11, episode 6); 'You've Got No Chutzpah' (series 11, episode 7)

*Said at the same time as Greg Davies, so does it count?

Judi Love

SERIES: 13

NUMBER OF TITLES: Five

NAMES OF EPISODES: 'I Think I've Got This' (series 13, episode 3); 'Shoe Who' (series 13, episode 4); 'Heg' (series 13, episode 7); 'You Tuper Super' (series 13, episode 8); 'House Queens' (series 13, episode 10)

Bob Mortimer

SERIES: 5 and Champions of Champions 1

NUMBER OF TITLES: Four

NAMES OF EPISODES: 'Residue Around the Hoof' (series 5, episode 4); 'A Wind-dried Puffin' (series 5, episode 5); 'Their Water's So Delicious' (series 5, episode 8); 'I've Sinned Again' (Champion of Champions 1, episode 2)

Victoria Coren Mitchell

SERIES: 12

NUMBER OF TITLES: Four

NAMES OF EPISODES: 'The Customised Inhaler' (series 12, episode 4); 'A Chair in a Sweet' (series 12, episode 6); 'The Integrity of the Product' (series 12, episode 7); 'Caring Uncle Minpict' (series 12, episode 10)

Fern Brady

SERIES: 14

NUMBER OF TITLES: Four

NAMES OF EPISODES: 'Dafty in the Middle' (series 14, episode 3); 'The System of Endless Plates' (series 14, episode 7); 'The One That Bats Do' (series 14, episode 8); 'Did I Meet These Potatoes Before?' (series 14, episode 10)

Ivo Graham

SERIES: 15

NUMBER OF TITLES: Four

NAMES OF EPISODES: 'The Curse of Politeness' (series 15, episode 1); 'I Love To Squander Promise' (series 15, episode 3); 'It's My Milk Now' (series 15, episode 6); 'A Yardstick for Failure' (series 15, episode 10)

MEGA TASKMASTER WORDSEARCH

Find the last names of the first 90 *Taskmaster* main series contestants.
Fastest wins.
Your time starts now.*

```
B R A N D T L F H M D M W C P K G D B U X K N A P P E T T H
H W V J B H J I L A A I A W Y Y I R M A B K B M U R R A Y B
E O U V E O O E U T V L N I J B L B W L R R M E K L R Y A N
R K B E C M N L D A I L G L K E B X F E A M A O A W T C O S
R O S G K A E D S F E I K K M J E G X S N A D B R U Z R A I
I M J A E S S I S E S C E I C W R O R H G C D R X D M J B D
N A W S T Z Q N U O H A Y N U I T R N E A K I I V E V O V I
G P F T T Z M G U P H N D S Q L L M B R N N X A N E D O N A
C A U D G L S L E V I N E O K L W A M O A A J I U E E L X T
P P D R C I K U M A R G K N G A Y N Y I T B Y N I Q N P C H
Z X E E F P B H O C V Q G T N N Z Z R U H R V G F N N M H O
D A W R F O E S C S O P A R K I N S O N A A B R R O I Y R W
U M L F I O F M O J M R Z C A L I L E O N D E A A P S M I A
P C U T V C P S B N R A E H P O C S Y R K Y A H M H Q A S R
H N U P Z Z H E T E T J N N M V X O K C O Z R A S J F A T D
I A C K E M P A F I R W B B M E H K N I E B É M A Z M C I K
L L J W D R A P R L R T U B G I V G E A N T I C Y P A A E E
L L L O U K K N A D P L O I O B T M A A T N T N L Z R S C C
I Y M Z K E W I H S S U I N R Y A C O M R Y E J S A T T O T
P X O N E N N A N D C O N N G E L D H H B N Y R B O I E O M
S C R I R D D L T S D O N X G L K E D E A L S M H A N R P C
M W T A B A G L L S Z Y E X C L A R Y I L M E S U F T M E H
S I I K L L Q R G F O S M I T H B O Y N E L M B I K W Q R A
V X M S G L S H F Y Y N R L R L C J H G F L H E V N J O P W
K P E G I E D R O Y C R I T C H I E P V I N E U D K H N F A
H D R I B K W K S A N D E R S M B C A M P B E L L U X A M W
A V C Y R W J T A R B U C K W I D D I C O M B E S W E F O A
N M O H A N L A N C G O C H A U D H R Y Q C H O W D H R Y O
M R O B I N S H R I Z W A N D B R O W N G A A L G P M G Z R
G O D L I M A N H Z C J D I O A I B U R C H T R L Z N E M J
```

* Visit taskmaster.tv/wordsearch for the answers.

GIVE ME SOME STATS:
What if things were *slightly* different?

History is full of 'what ifs'. What if Abraham Lincoln hadn't been assassinated? What if the USSR had got to the moon first? What if the main character from *Grand Theft Auto* was played by a mid-30s comedian from Kettering? *Taskmaster* is no different. But thanks to statistics, we can look into the alternate worlds of what would have happened if certain decisions had gone a different way.

Hypothesis 1
If James Acaster had been in any other series, he would have won.

WHERE DOES THIS COME FROM?
On multiple appearances on podcasts (specifically the official *Taskmaster Podcast*), James claims the contestants on his series were preternaturally talented and that, if he had been given a fractionally less competent cast, he would have sailed to victory.

WHAT DO THE STATS SAY?
Almost certainly incorrect. James Acaster scored 165 points in his series, which is not bad – he scored more points than nine of the previous champions. But he has a points-per-task score of 3.06, which is decidedly average – it's below 36 other contestants and 16 of the 17 champions.

12 / A SHOW ABOUT PEDANTRY

WHAT SERIES WOULD JAMES HAVE DONE BEST IN?

Series 1, the only one where his score is higher than every other contestant.

WHAT SERIES WOULD JAMES HAVE DONE WORST IN?

Series 12, where he would have finished bottom.

IS THERE ANY METRIC WHERE JAMES ACASTER COMES AHEAD OF ED GAMBLE?

He was fractionally better at live tasks than Ed, scoring 2.50 points per live task ahead of Ed's 2.40.

ARE JAMES' EYES ACTUALLY CIRCLES?

According to Wikipedia, the human eye is approximately spherical in shape.

Hypothesis 2

If Greg hadn't sided with Mae Martin on a few key decisions, they wouldn't have won series 15.

WHERE DOES THIS COME FROM?

Several controversial arguments arose in series 15: Mae Martin claimed to 'throw' a ball that they had attached to a piece of string, an assertion to which the rest of their colleagues took offence. In a later task, Mae drew several pineapples on a piece of paper to win the 'most pineapples' task as Greg accepted their argument.

WHAT DO THE STATS SAY?
Mixed. On the one hand, Mae won their series by 16 points, the second highest margin of victory ever, so even if they were disqualified in both of those tasks (and everyone else was bumped up one), they still had a good cushion there – they would have finished on 164 points, 4 points ahead of the nearest challenger (Kiell Smith-Bynoe).

BUT ...
It's worth saying that if Mae had been disqualified in the drum task, they would have been 12 points behind the leader, Jenny Eclair. No contestant has ever been that far behind the leader after four episodes and gone on to win the show. Whether that massive margin would have affected them in the studio tasks, we'll never know!

IS A JERK A TYPE OF THROW?
We are not opening that can of worms again.

Hypothesis 3
If team tasks weren't scored so strangely in series 1, Josh Widdicombe wouldn't have won.

WHERE DOES THIS COME FROM?
The show was still working out the scoring kinks in series 1 and, as such, team tasks weren't 5 points split between the two teams. Instead the teams were given 2 points for a win and 0 or 1 for a defeat. Given how close series 1 was (the top three were all separated by a single point), it's a fair question ...

12 / A SHOW ABOUT PEDANTRY

WHAT DO THE STATS SAY?
Almost certainly. Frank Skinner's team won two of their team tasks, and it seems likely that under conventional team task scoring they would have got at least 4 or 5 points for their final task, and the other team either 0 or 1, given that Greg called the team of three's attempt 'The worst acting I've ever seen committed to film.' Therefore, Frank would have scored a total of 95 or 96 points, pipping Josh to the post.

IS THAT THE ONLY CONTROVERSY IN SERIES 1?
Understandably, given how close the series was, there's also a scandal around the 'individual' task for the series, where Josh counted beans, spaghetti hoops and rice for a bonus point, which ultimately won him the series. This was repeated in series 12, where Greg gave Morgana Robinson a bonus point for calling Alex a 'little f***er' in the first episode, which proved to be the margin of victory for her at the end of the series …

DID JOSH, ALEX, TIM AND FRANK EVER MAKE IT TO THEIR LOVELY POST-SHOW HOLIDAY TO COLOGNE?
Yes, it was delightful.

TASKMASTER HALL OF GLORY

Greatest Contestant EVER Statistically

NAME: John Robins

SERIES POINTS: 192 (3.84 points per task)

SERIES: 17

POSITION IN SERIES: First by some distance (sorry Joanne)

FUN FACTS: John Robins scored 3 or more in every filmed task in his series, apart from one (the task where he had to stick the heaviest item to the board, where he was disqualified). In objectively judged tasks, John scored 4.04 – the highest ever. By episode 9, John had scored 174 points – that's as many as all but three of the other contestants had managed in ten episodes. John never scored fewer than 17 in an episode – this is the highest minimum score anyone has ever achieved.

GREATEST ACHIEVEMENT: Painting Freddie Mercury onto the back of his head.

LOWEST MOMENT: When Greg and Alex made him sweat pretending that he had been disqualified in several tasks (he hadn't, they're just horrible people).

RELEVANT QUOTE: 'Are you … a cable?' – John, trying to work out who or what could be following him if they're not a person and they have a gender

12 / A SHOW ABOUT PEDANTRY

Edinburgh Task 11: How Did It Go?

By this stage of the competition, people were visibly tiring. They had their own Edinburgh shows to prepare for and they'd been doing stupid things for me for months. We would eventually learn that a year-long competition was too long for humans. We don't have that capacity. Also, 20 people are far too many for nearly all situations. Five contestants doing tasks for a few months is just about manageable.

And so it turned out that only Tim FitzHigham found me skulking in London Zoo. In fact, at the time I thought I was completely alone because Mr FitzHigham had decided to stalk me, to secretly photograph me and never said hello, Acaster-style.

I was genuinely surprised by the sly photos he revealed during the show in Edinburgh. It's always good when contestants take the upper hand and make up their own rules.

EDINBURGH TASK 12
5 August 2010

Morning all,

So, it's August. We're nearly there. As you know, the results will be revealed in the Pleasance Queen Dome, Edinburgh, on Friday 27 August, just after midnight (so, actually, very early on the Saturday morning). Hope you can make it – it's actually already very nearly sold out, so if you haven't yet, please let me know if you want any comps.

Meanwhile, here is your FINAL CHALLENGE:

YOU BET

Please tell me what position (out of 20) you think you will finish then ...

Have a bet on who you think will win the *Taskmaster*. I am the Bookmaker (as well as the Taskmaster) and you can put on as much or as little money as you like. As before, the banking details are Barclays, account number 12345678, sort code XX-XX-XX. The only tricky thing for you is that you won't know the odds until later. So bet wisely. Here are the twenty runners:

Mr T. FitzHigham
Mr M. Watson
Mr T. Wrigglesworth

12 / A SHOW ABOUT PEDANTRY

Mr T. Basden

Mr M. Wozniak

Mr J. Dowdeswell

Mr A. Pitcher

Ms J. Long

Mr D. Atkinson

Mr L. Woolf

Mr G. Morgan

Mr J. Wilkinson

Mr H. Wehn

Mr S. Hall

Mr J. Christmas

Mr M. Olver

Mr R. Edwards

Mr T. Key

Mr L. Langford

Mr S. Goldsmith

Just tell me who you think will win and how much you're betting (as well as what position you think you'll come).

Thank you.

See you on 27 August.

Good luck.

TM

THE WINNER

Edinburgh Task 12: How Did It Go?

I can't condone gambling, but I can tell you that 13 of the 20 competitors were in attendance in Edinburgh (the other seven featured on the screen) and after a nod-off tiebreak (nodding the most in a minute), Tim FitzHigham came second behind the present-day Junior Taskmaster's Assistant, Mr Mike Wozniak. Neither betted on themselves, thankfully.

Further details are, for now at least, delightfully lost. Social media hadn't taken over our hands and minds back then. We didn't record everything that happened. Many of the task attempts are now merely memories that some of us dredge up fondly when we meet in pubs, far too infrequently.

I don't know who came third or last. I don't know how Tim Key did, except that thankfully he didn't win. I just remember a wild joy that night in the Queen Dome, Bristo Square, Edinburgh. The audience, participants and I were all drawn into this sprawling binfire. It was an accident. We hadn't planned any of it. But a tiny spark from nowhere took hold of us comedians and is still burning bright today.

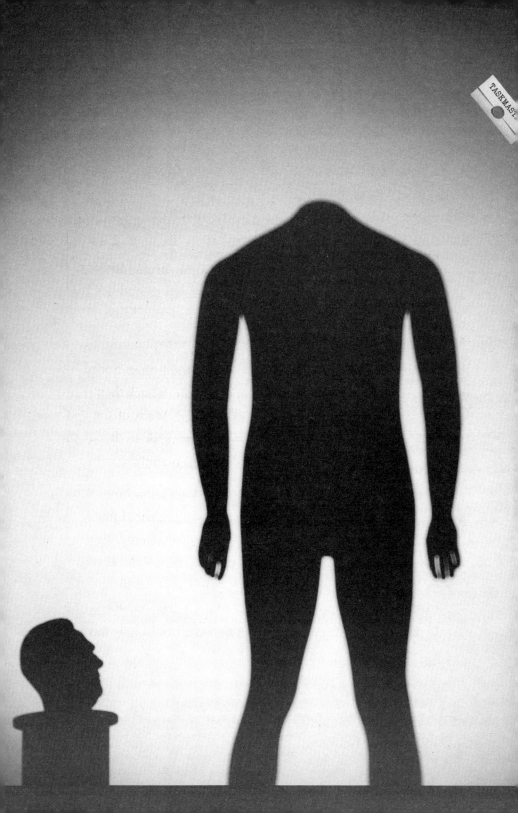

INDEX

Acaster, James 50, 54, 148, 149, 216, 236, 257, 290–1
   circular eyes 114, 291
Adefope, Lolly 10, 42, 114–15, 122, 147
animals and children, tasks with 262–4
arguments, most contested tasks 141–5
Atkinson, Dan 5, 127, 154
audience, the studio 28, 144
Avalon, production company 6

Backshall, Steve 269
Baddiel, David 26, 84, 89, 102, 140, 149, 167–8, 170, 226, 240, 259
baked beans 45, 107, 214, 216
Basden, Tom 5, 61, 228–30, 273
Bea, Aisling 31, 45, 48, 54, 70, 88, 124, 200, 212, 235, 254–5
Beaumont, Lucy (-fer the Rock God) 42, 51, 52, 53, 69, 152, 173
Beckett, Rob 75, 88, 134, 142, 196, 199, 241, 243, 255
birthplaces, contestant 78, 88–9
   proximity to the coast and chances of winning *Taskmaster* 80–1
Blake-Lobb, James 176–7
Boyle, Frankie 41, 71, 82, 88, 102, 113, 126, 144–5, 146, 172
Brady, Fern 88, 102, 106, 150, 151, 239, 288
Brand, Jo 41, 102, 149, 172, 244, 259
Brown, Doc 47, 97
Burch, Desiree 33, 51, 85–6, 89, 124, 126, 201, 238, 263

Campbell (aka Doctor Cigarettes), Sam 51, 69, 81, 89, 92, 102, 110, 151–2, 212, 233, 239, 241, 243, 264
Carol 258
Cartwright, Andy 12, 58, 256, 257, 262

Champion of Champions 1, 49, 125, 166–7, 170, 182, 234, 244, 245, 286, 287
Champions 1, 11, 80–1, 90–2, 170, 210–11, 240–5, 290–2
Channel 4 11, 12
Chaudry, Asim 54, 138, 202, 245, 258
Chawawa (aka the Bernard Basher), Munya 79, 87, 103, 138, 150, 151, 238
cheating 28, 133–9
'chicken' 112
chickpea cult 226
children and animals, tasks with 262–4
Chiles, Adrian 266
Chowdry, Paul 47, 76, 123, 142, 196
   bouncy castle, individual task 108
Christie, Bridget 28, 60, 65, 85, 103, 160, 171, 173, 238
Christmas, Jarred 5, 248
circles *see* Acaster eyes, James
Clapham Grand theatre 24
Clark, Rylan 267
Clary (aka Butch), Julian 35, 45, 56, 69, 83, 89, 152, 239
cocktails, *Taskmaster* 208–9
Conaty, Roisin 29, 46, 72–3, 94, 97, 141, 158, 159, 188, 203, 212, 247
Cooper, Daisy May 26, 32, 85, 113, 169, 182, 208, 236, 237
Coren Mitchell, Victoria 50, 82, 170, 198, 201, 282, 287
Coughlan, Nicola 267, 268
COVID-19 lockdown hometasks 116–20, 237–8
crew at the *Taskmaster* house 57–9, 71, 226

Dave TV channel 11–12
Davies, Alan 192–3, 198, 237, 263, 282

INDEX

Davies, Greg 7
   birthplace 78, 88
   hatred of football 195–8
   Mad Helmet Murderer game 47
   Mel Giedroyc's impossible task 109
   nicknames for Alex 283–5
   portrait 41
   series introductions 19–20
   wooden puppet 53
Dennis, Hugh 30, 41, 88, 102, 189, 196, 200–1, 257
Dent, Susie 140, 281–2
Devonshire, Andy 6, 8–9, 23, 58
Dillon, James 24
Dimoldenberg, Amelia 267
disqualifications 1, 67, 71, 73, 74, 124, 126, 133–6, 138–9, 142, 173, 265
   least and most disqualified contestants 146
Dowdeswell, James 5, 183, 231
Dracula *see* Mohammed, Nick
Duker, Sophie 26, 49, 103, 122–3, 171, 238, 241, 242, 245

Eclair, Jenny 52, 56, 71, 88, 105, 144–5, 172, 238, 244, 292
Edinburgh Fringe festival, *Taskmaster* at the 2–6
   Emergency Task 251, 273
   John Scales 129
   Sports Relief 129
   Task 1: Money Fun 13, 36
   Task 2: Find a Hedgehog 36–7, 61
   Task 3: Name Your Rivals and Here Comes the Sun 62–3, 98
   Task 4: Massive Christmas Presents 99, 127
   Task 5: Bumper Boy 128–9, 154
   Task 6: Alex Horne is a Magnificent Man 155, 183
   Task 7: The Drinking Race 184–5, 203
   Task 8: A Lovely Love Song 203–5, 228–30

   Task 9: What fruit is Alex holding? 231–2, 248
   Task 10: Half an Hour in Hong Kong 250, 270–2
   Task 11: Where's Ally? 274–5, 295
   Task 12: You Bet 296–8
Edwards, Rick 5, 61
eggs
   facts 112, 140, 174, 213, 265, 280
   Romesh Ranganathan's irrational hatred of 265

Farah, Sir Mo 46, 199, 266, 268, 269
fastest task attempts 199–201
Fielding (aka the Clock Tamperer), Noel 30, 47, 96, 97, 136, 147–8, 190, 235–6, 242, 245
fire hazards 54–6
FitzHigham, Tim 5, 295, 298
Flossie, Alex's niece 264
food tasks 147–8, 208–9, 212–14, 216–20, 222–6
Fred the Swede 93–5, 226
friendship *see* truth

Gamble, Ed 26, 43, 146, 149, 150, 212, 226, 236, 240, 241, 243, 244, 291
   longest and worst task attempt EVER 125
Geoff, the Former Traffic Warden 257
Gibson, Sian 25, 54, 88, 143
Giedroyc, Mel 44, 66, 75, 102, 153, 235
   Chocolate Club Sandwich 147–8, 219–20
   Hide the ball from Alex, individual task 109
Gilbert, Rhod 28, 45, 50, 78, 88, 121, 146, 148, 183, 236
'girdle' 112
Godliman, Kerry 50, 54, 81, 148, 168, 172, 173, 210, 236, 242, 243, 257
Goldsmith, Stuart 5, 98, 127, 183, 185
Gorman (aka Pea Taker and Tea Splosher), Dave 75–6, 196, 199, 256, 264

INDEX

Skull and Crossbones Surprise recipe 218–19
Graham, Ivo 87, 88, 102, 113, 144–5, 146, 165–6, 170, 171, 288
greeting Alex 113–15
Guru-Murthy, Krishnan 56

hacks, task 158–60, 257, 281
hair facts and stats 243–6
Hall, Steve 5, 231
Hannah, John 267
Herring, Richard 26, 41, 101, 113, 170, 182, 208, 240, 245
history of the world 171–3
hometasking tasks, COVID-19 lockdown 116–20
Horne, Alex
   birthplace 78
   Brown Peacocks short story 278–9
   day-in-the-life at the *Taskmaster* house 57–9
   erotic fan fiction 285
   fatherhood 2, 6, 175–6, 191
   fish puns contest 109–10, 214
   Fred the Blusher 93–5
   gets annoyed 60
   greeting Alex 113–15
   honorary doctorate 178–81
   lies about his height 6
   nicknames 283–5
   nudity 175
   School Tasking 175–7, 180–1
   task participation 70, 75, 86, 147–8, 158, 159–60, 167, 171, 172, 173, 192–3, 212, 226, 257, 268
      terrible things he has eaten on the show 159–60, 212
   working with Andy Devonshire 8–9
Horne Section 93–4
horse facts 188
house and grounds, the *Taskmaster* 39–43, 44–5
   bathroom and shower room 41, 42
   the caravan 44–5
   day-in-the-life at 57–8

entrance hall and reception room 41, 42
fire hazards 54–6
Greg's portrait 41
laboratory and kitchen 41, 42
layout diagrams 43, 45
Howard, Russell 191, 197, 199–200, 214, 258
Hugh the Gentleman 256

imaginary friends 41, 89
inconsistent contestant, most 60
individual bespoke tasks 107–11, 142
international superstars 90–2
invitation and concept letter, *Taskmaster* 2–5

Junior Taskmaster 89

Kalyan (the Magician), Gareth Simon 258–9
Kearns, John 45, 52, 78, 102, 106, 150, 151, 261
Kendall, Sarah 55, 85, 89, 237–8, 241, 243, 244
Key (aka the Bathtub Fiddler), Tim 2, 5, 7, 29, 36, 61, 69–70, 93, 94, 97, 133–4, 141–2, 158, 188, 203, 212, 234, 248, 271, 273, 293, 298
   Citrus Faeces recipe 217–18
Khan, Guz 33, 124, 245, 263, 282
Knappett, Jessica 48, 50, 55, 149, 173, 192, 210, 257
   falls off the stage 15, 26, 43
Kumar, Nish 54, 70, 124, 214, 254, 255

lab contestant, best 202
Langford, Lloyd 5, 36, 203, 231, 270
Leshurr, Lady 266
Levine, Alice 86, 87, 113, 197, 244
Long, Rosie 5, 183
longest tasks 29–31
   the best 121–3
   other important and surprisingly long attempts 126

INDEX

the worst 123–5
    the worst EVER 125
losers, biggest 87, 247
Love, Judi 85, 95, 103, 121, 160, 171, 245, 287
    Tower of Love recipe 223–4
Lycett, Joe 41, 54, 75, 97, 114, 147, 183

Mack, Lee 41, 45, 55, 67, 73, 74, 238, 241
Maddix, Jamali 44, 45, 55, 74–5, 84, 173, 237
    Full Day Set-Up recipe 222–3
map of the world, according to *Taskmaster* 88–9
Marco the cute dog 263
Martin, Mae 53, 80, 82, 89, 90, 105, 144–5, 146, 166, 167, 170, 171, 241, 243, 291–2
    understudy (*see* Smith-Bynoe, Kiell)
Matafeo, Rose 84, 89, 149, 150, 226, 237
Mayor of Chesham's testicles, Peter Hudson 255
McNally, Joanne 48, 49, 88, 90–1, 104, 194
Meaden, Deborah 266, 267
Millican, Sarah 42, 55–6, 80, 103, 150, 151, 227, 261
Mohammed, Nick 15, 79, 115, 239, 240, 265
Morgan, Guy 5
Mortimer, Bob 48, 54, 78, 79, 88, 157, 197, 241, 254–5, 287
    Residue Around the Hoof Marmite recipe 220
Murray, Al 47, 75–6, 77, 97, 134, 135, 142, 183, 243
mute pervert *see* Herring, Richard

Nell the toddler 262–3
New Years' Treats, *Taskmaster* 10, 12, 46, 56, 266–9
nightmare, f∗∗∗ing *see* Rosalind

Ó Briain, Dara 25, 80, 88, 102, 106, 150, 151, 172, 198, 216, 238, 241, 243–4, 261
off-site tasks 66–77
    see also transportation tasks
O'Hanlon, Ardal 33–4, 51, 85, 88, 95, 173, 245, 260
Ol' Goosebump Arm *see* Coren Mitchell, Victoria
oldest contestant 35
Olver, Mark 5, 61, 275
Osman, Richard 54, 102, 106, 212, 281
outfits, *Taskmaster* contestant 57, 60, 233
    Actual Fashion 237
    the Advent of the Boilersuit 235–6
    champions and clothing colour stats 240–2
    the Comfort Years 237–8
    the Costume Years 236
    Maximalist High Art 238–9
    the M&S Jumper Years 234–5
    Return of Normcore 239

Parkinson, Katherine 66, 78, 87, 146, 168–9, 174, 208, 237, 243
Pascoe, Sara 75–6, 135, 143, 199, 234, 256
Patatas the cat 43
Peacock, Jonnie 266
peacocks, brown 278–9
Pemberton, Steve 34, 51, 194, 265
Perkins, Sue 51, 52, 83, 146, 173, 239
    public breakdown over flatulence 152
    Surprisingly Pleasant Fish Sausages recipe 225
Phillips, Sally 54, 88, 89, 115, 126, 172, 190–1, 200, 212, 214, 254–5
    fish puns, individual task 109
Pinewood Studios 24
pitch to TV channels 16–18, 21–2
Pitcher, Al 5, 36, 231
prize tasks 10
    biggest losers 87
    football themed prizes 195–8
    greatest prize – Steve Pemberton's cryptic *Guardian* crossword

INDEX

hair as a prize 244
Joanne McNally's Che Guevara
    balloon 91
least age-appropriate gift 267
most and least expensive 267
'Most cash' Edinburgh Fringe Festival
    task 10
most dead person brought in 268
most successful contestants 32–4
recycled prizes 46–8, 50–3
public participation, unplanned 66, 67–8,
    69, 72, 73, 76, 77, 183

Quentin 259–60

Radical, Kojey 267, 268
Ramsey, Chris 26, 78, 84–5, 97, 173, 193,
    227
Ranganathan, Romesh 29, 47, 72–3, 94,
    97, 141, 158, 188, 195, 203, 240
    irrational hatred of eggs 265
recipes, *Taskmaster* 208–9, 217–20, 222–5
recycled props 46–53
Richardson, Jon 97, 102, 106, 255
    William Tell Overture individual task
    108
Ritchie, Charlotte 55, 73, 84, 173, 212,
    237
Rizwan (aka the Sneaky Pasta Snake),
    Mawaan 32, 81, 85, 88, 137–8, 146,
    159–60, 169, 174, 209, 237, 242
Robins, John 28, 56, 80–1, 82, 86, 104,
    170, 173, 194, 210, 239, 240, 241,
    244–5, 294
Robinson, Morgana 81, 85, 87, 89, 91,
    124, 170, 210, 244, 245, 263, 282,
    285, 293
Rosalind 157, 214, 254–5
rubber ducks 1, 66, 78, 81, 200–1
Rush, Lenny 10, 266, 267, 269
Ryan, Katherine 89, 91–2, 243, 255

Sanders, Lou 44, 55, 80, 83, 143, 191–2,
    210, 236, 241, 243, 262
    Dust à la Fizz Wizz recipe 222

Sausage Studies 161–5
School Tasking 175–7, 180–1
scores, *Taskmaster*
    greatest contestant ever statistically 294
    highest and lowest scores on New
        Years' Treats 266–7
    highest in a solo filmed task 227
    highest in an episode 106
    highest solo task score 261
    lowest in a series 247
    lowest in an episode 153
    most episode wins 182
'show zero' 25
Sinha, Paul 126, 143, 192, 262
Skinner, Frank 7, 46, 47, 72–3, 94, 97, 142,
    158, 159, 188, 240, 293
'small nasally one' *see* Widdicombe, Josh
Smith-Bynoe, Kiell 41, 71, 78, 82, 89, 105,
    131, 144–5, 146, 166–7, 172, 238,
    243, 292
    Cowering Kenyan Bench recipe 224
spirit animal, *Taskmaster see* rubber ducks
sporty tasks 189–94, 199–200
stage, the *Taskmaster* studio 26, 28
stats, show
    about New Years' Treats 266–9
    being a vegan and chances of winning
        Taskmaster 210–11
    being born by the sea and chances of
        winning *Taskmaster* 80–1
    colour to wear for best chance of
        winning *Taskmaster* 240–2
    going to university and chances of
        winning *Taskmaster* 170
    hair facts and stats 243–6
    what if things were *slightly* different?
        290–1
Stirling, Iain 41, 83, 88, 143, 144, 146
Struthers, Ali 176–7
studio, the *Taskmaster* 15, 23–8
    layout diagram 27
stupidest moments 165–9

Tarbuck, Liza 68, 78, 170, 199, 200, 202,
    240, 245, 286

INDEX

Taskmaster beginning
   Alex's invitation and concept letter 2–5
   first series commissioned 11
   journey from stage to screen 6–7, 11–12
   'show zero' 25
   the studio 15, 23–8
   testing the tasks 23
   the TV channel pitch 16–18, 21–2
   see also Edinburgh Fringe festival, *Taskmaster* at the
Taskmaster Education 175–7
Taskmaster Hotel 78, 102
Taskmaster Podcast 60, 68, 140, 210
Taylor, Rebecca Lucy 266
teamwork, *Taskmaster* 72, 102
   Aisling Bea, Bob Mortimer, Sally Phillips 254–5
   impact of strange scoring 292–3
   John Robins, Joanne McNally, Sophie Willan 104
   Liza Tarbuck, Tim Vine, Asim Chaudry 202
   longest and worst task attempts 124–5
   Mae Martin, Kiell Smith-Bynoe, Jenny Eclair 105
   Nish Kumar, Mark Watson 254, 255
   sabotage 241
   Sam Campbell, Julian Clary, Lucy Beaumont 102
   Sarah Millican, Munya Chawawa 103
   songs for Rosalind 254–5
   Sophie Duker, Bridget Christie, Judi Love 103–4
Thomas, Joe 83, 87, 143–4, 244, 262
thrones 28
titles, *Taskmaster* episode 286–8
Tomlinson, Gabby 259
transportation tasks 82–6
truth *see* friendship
two-part tasks 147–52

urinators of the British Isles 78, 79

Vegas, Johnny 50, 67–8, 85, 146, 173, 208, 237
Vine, Tim 74, 126, 200, 202, 236, 243, 244, 280
vole charisma 55
Vorderman, Carol 267

Wang, Phil 23, 45, 50, 89, 146, 148, 170, 216, 236, 240, 280
Watson, Mark 5, 30–1, 32, 36, 54, 61, 70–1, 88, 126, 183, 199, 214, 231, 248, 254, 255
Wayne the air dancer 50–1
Wehn, Henning 5, 98, 129, 183, 270
Widdicombe, Josh 11, 29, 35, 94, 97, 141, 142, 158–9, 188, 195, 210, 216, 234, 239, 240, 247, 292–3
   bean counting, individual task 107, 214, 293
Wilkinson, Joe 5, 26, 146, 203, 231, 235, 255, 270, 281
   public breakdown over a potato 139
Willan, Sophie 28, 52–3, 78, 104, 194, 241, 243
Winkleman, Claudia 41, 96, 266, 267, 268, 269
Winter, Vicky 12
Wix, Katy 44, 88, 89, 149, 168, 259
Wokoma, Susan 56, 83, 92, 111, 152, 264
Woolf, Lloyd 5, 270
Wordsearch, *Taskmaster* 289
Wozniak, Mike 5, 36, 55, 73, 82–3, 127, 203, 231, 244, 248, 286, 298
   farting on an airplane, individual task 110
Wrigglesworth, Tom 5, 129
Wright, Jennifer Christine 256–7

youngest contestant 10

ACKNOWLEDGEMENTS

Alex

Taskmaster has always been a team effort. Team is literally part of the word itself, as are Mattress, Karate and Arses, so it must be true. Apologies if you don't see your name here but you've helped make the show over the years; please know that I am grateful but forgetful. You are almost certainly a crucial cog in our noisy machine.

I would therefore like to thank every person who has ever worked on the show, both in front of the camera, behind the camera and in different rooms and buildings to where the cameras are. There are simply too many to mention here but I would like to particularly credit Andrew Dames and Amy Tuckwell for all the extra time and love they pour into what we do.

Sticking with names beginning with A, Andy Devonshire has made this book beautiful thanks to a level of dedication I am in awe of, and Andy Cartwright's sense of language and humour has been as vital here as it has been for the past ten years. And Vicky Winter, who is the one who sorts everything out, should always be thanked whenever possible. You're the best.

Having Greg as my Taskmaster is still the biggest thrill in my working life. He's the funniest person I've ever sat next to. I'm proud and insistent that we are now friends. And I'm immensely grateful to every other comedian or celebrity who has set aside their pride and had fun with us on the show.

ACKNOWLEDGEMENTS

Thank you too to James Taylor and Mary-Grace Brunker for making this book happen, and everyone else at Avalon who contributes so much to such a silly thing, particularly Florrie Sheehan and Jack Pelling who always do so with what seem to be genuine smiles on their faces. I would also like to mention both Channel 4 and UKTV who have enabled us to task for such a long time and have never once questioned anything I have written. To allow and encourage ridiculous ideas is a rare thing in telly and much appreciated.

Our publishers, Quercus, have been unbelievably understanding about the oddness of the material within this book. Thanks first to Jane Sturrock for suggesting the book, to Victoria Millar for somehow pulling all the strings together, to Carrie Hutchison for the audio, Ella Horne (no relation but GREAT name) for the marketing, Elizabeth Masters and Myrto Kalevrezou for the publicity, and everyone else there who has helped the book emerge. Behind the scenes, Jonathan Baker did the design, Matthew Everett sorted out the production, Lisa Hughes did the copyedit, Philippa Wilkinson the proofread and Kate Inskip the index – thank you all.

To Jack Bernhardt I want to say, sorry for dragging you into this. The reader will never know the extent to which your brain capacity has been taken up by the many stupid things that we have done. During filming, I'm always grateful and embarrassed about how much menial work the runners and researchers have to do on a daily basis. We comics have all the fun without the clearing up. Jack now seems to be in charge of the theoretical clearing up: sorting the data,

ACKNOWLEDGEMENTS

counting the points and ducks and making sense of the nonsense. Thanks Jack. Thack.

Finally, if you're still reading this then I want to thank YOU. The people who watch *Taskmaster*, in my experience – which is daily and always welcome and wonderful – are good people. They/you are interesting, interested, international but never interchangeable. You're odd and silly and patient. We have always felt that this is a collaborative show, somehow, one with unintended consequences, like *Taskmaster*-related stags, hens and weddings, school/girl-guide/cub-scout *Taskmaster* groups, amazing *Taskmaster* tribute art and music, and general enthusiasm and support for our world. Without you, it'd be a far more soulless endeavour.

Jack

I still cannot quite believe I have been allowed to co-write a book about one of my favourite ever shows, and there are a lot of people to thank/blame for this coming about. Thank you to everyone who works on the show, and especially to the excellent Andy Cartwright and brilliant Vicky Winter for fielding my many, many, many questions about the Taskmaster house and giving in to my demands to see every transcript of every show.

A lot of the content for this book came out of *Taskmaster The People's Podcast*, and without that show I can't imagine I'd be writing this today, so thank you to current producer Christine Macdonald and former producer Ben Drayton – both have had to put up with my failure to understand a microphone every week – and also

ACKNOWLEDGEMENTS

my incredible co-hosts Jenny Eclair and Lou Sanders, who have tolerated this statistical nerdery with varying degrees of enthusiasm/frustration. Thank you to every fellow *Taskmaster* obsessive who has written into the podcast to ask a question – so many sections in this book only came about because of the weird and wonderful suggestions people make each week.

Thank you also to my gorgeous family, Valerie, Camille and Zoe. I love you all very much (and am sorry I talk about you all too much on the podcast).

Thank you to my terrific agent Katie Williams at The Agency and thank you to everyone at Avalon, especially James Taylor for commissioning the podcast in the first place. I should also thank Toby Moses at the *Guardian*, who saw my lockdown-induced ramblings about *Taskmaster* on my blog and decided to turn it into an article, which led, eventually, to all this. I'm still very confused about how I got here.

Lastly, a big thank you to Big (because he is, actually) Alex Horne for writing this very silly book with me, and for being so generous with his time and energy. I'm incredibly honoured to be a tiny part of this fantastic thing that brings joy to so many people, and I hope I haven't ruined it with too many statistics (as I am wont to do).